Super Joe

Super Joe

THE LIFE AND LEGEND OF JOE CHARBONEAU

Joe Charboneau
with
Burt Graeff and Terry Pluto

STEIN AND DAY/*Publishers*/New York

First published in 1981
Copyright © 1981 by Joe Charboneau, Burt Graeff, Terry Pluto
All rights reserved
Designed by L.A.Ditizio
Printed in the United States of America
STEIN AND DAY/ *Publishers*
Scarborough House
Briarcliff Manor, N.Y. 10510

Library of Congress Cataloging in Publication Data

Charboneau, Joe.
    Super Joe.

    1. Charboneau, Joe.   2. Baseball players—
United States—Biography.   I. Graeff, Burt.
II. Pluto, Terry, 1955–   .   III. Title.
GV865.C43A37   796.357 '092 '4   [B]   81-6169
ISBN 0-8128-2806-2   AACR2

PREFACE

Well, it's hard to believe what a wonderful year 1980 has been for me. Just playing in the Major Leagues was a fulfilling experience. I've made many lasting friendships, including a great group of teammates, tremendously supportive fans, some understanding reporters, but none closer than my agent, Dan Donnelly. The thrill of the Rookie of the Year Award was indescribable, especially because I had promised my wife, Cindy, that I would win it for her if I made the Majors.

Now, I can enjoy and appreciate the good things that happened and look forward to a rewarding career. I only hope that I can continue to bring the great fans of Cleveland something to cheer about. To all of them, a special thank you.

—Joe Charboneau

CONTENTS

The Big Leagues

Afterword

ACKNOWLEDGMENTS

We would like to thank Karen Ahearn, who introduced agent Dan Donnelly to editor Art Ballant. Without her, this book might not have been published.

We would also like to thank Kathleen Charboneau, Art Charboneau, Dan Donnelly, Cindy Charboneau, Frank Lucy, Eddie Bockman and Bob Quinn for their assistance.

Super Joe

The Beginning

ORIGINS

The church was dark and quiet. The only light came from the flickering yellow candles around the altar. A pregnant Kathleen Charboneau was on her knees. She was making a novena to the Mother of Perpetual Help. On this day in St. James Roman Catholic Church of Belvedere, Illinois, Kathleen Charboneau made a pact with her Lord. The result of that deal would be Joseph Charboneau, a man they would later call Super Joe. This Super Joe Charboneau would become the 1980 American League Rookie of the Year as a member of the Cleveland Indians.

Kathleen Charboneau was not praying for base hits. That was yet to come. No, she was asking for a little divine intervention into her husband's career. Times had been tough for Art Charboneau. He had spent seven years as a milkman. After a spell of unemployment, Art Charboneau was working in the unrewarding field of selling shoes. The bills were high and the income low. It was a time to pray for something, anything which would be better.

"I prayed for Art to get a good job," said Kathleen Charboneau. "I said that I would name my next child Joseph or Mary depending upon what the baby was. I would name it after a member of the Holy Family in hopes that God would help Art."

15

The child she was carrying at the time of her promise became Joseph Charboneau. He has no middle name, in the same way that Jesus' father was known only as Joseph. The Charboneaus' next child was a girl who was called Mary. And yes, Art Charboneau did find his successful niche in the world of work.

"For a while, everything came out great," said Kathleen Charboneau. "But the night Joe was born was something else. There was nothing easy about it."

The birth of Super Joe reflects his baseball career. There were starts and stops, frustration and then incredible joy.

Art and Kathleen Charboneau lived in Belvedere. It was an Illinois farm town of about 10,000 in 1955. At that time, the Charboneaus had three boys and a girl. The boys were stallions, the oldest being 12. When they went to the store, it was not uncommon for havoc to reign, as cans would roll down the aisle and fruit would be hurled about. One merchant never forgave them for reducing his pickle display to rubble, as the floor was stewed in glass, juice and pickles.

"When the time was near for Joe to be born, my parents and Art's both offered to take Carol, our girl, but neither side of the family wanted the boys," recalled Kathleen Charboneau. "The grandparents were good to the kids, but I didn't want to stick one side with the boys when they thought they were rowdy. So I kept the whole family together and at home with me."

On the night of June 16, 1955, Kathleen Charboneau knew that she was ready to deliver. She hoped to make it until morning when the grandparents could be summoned to watch the children.

"At 3 A.M., I told Art that we had to go to the hospital," said Kathleen. A neighbor was imported to babysit, while Kathleen and Art departed in a pickup truck. As they drove to the hospital, they were followed by a local merchant who had just finished closing a bar. The truck's rear lights were broken, and this fellow continually rammed his Ford into the back of the Charboneau truck.

At this point, Joseph Charboneau was taking more knocks than he would as a shirtless, bare-fisted boxcar fighter slugging it out and getting his face bloodied by Mexican migrant workers.

"Every time the guy hit our truck, I was really jarred," said Kathleen. "Finally, Art got so mad he stopped the truck and went out to fight the man. I told him to forget it and just drive me to the hospital."

As the Charboneaus motored up a hill, they spotted the hospital. Suddenly, they were stopped by a roadblock. The road was being worked on, so the truck was forced to turn around, and they had to drive two extra miles to reach their destination.

Kathleen Charboneau finally arrived at the hospital at 3:40 A.M. A nun helped her to a bed, and Kathleen promptly gave birth to Joe with no doctor present. The 8-pound 10½-ounce baby boy was brought into the world by the nun.

"It was a strange thing," said Kathleen. "There was only one other baby in the nursery at the time. It belonged to our doctor, Dr. O'Malley, who had just become a father. He got to me right after Joe was born."

The circumstances of Joe's birth created a special relationship between the mother and son.

"I have had seven children and there is this certain closeness I have with Joe that is not there with the others," said Kathleen. "After he was born, I had him in my arms constantly that first year. The doctors said that Joe had a traumatic experience because I tried to hold him in for so long. At the time, I was emotionally upset because of the strain of the children and the money problems. But when I held Joe, I felt so good, so wonderful."

Kathleen and Art Charboneau met on New Year's Eve of 1941 in Rockford, Illinois. Kathleen was a telephone operator. When she got off work, she usually walked to the center of town with a girlfriend. Once, on their way, they were offered a ride by a boy Kathleen knew. The other fellow in the car was Art Charboneau.

"At the time, I was engaged to a man who was stationed in Pearl Harbor," said Kathleen. "The fellow driving the car asked me for a date the next day. I accepted. I set Art up with another girlfriend of mine."

Those two couples double-dated for three weeks. One day, Art's girlfriend and Kathleen's boyfriend grew ill. So Art took out Kathleen. They were engaged in June of 1942 and married on September

26, 1942. Their first child, Joe's older brother Art, would arrive on December 15, 1943.

And what happened to the serviceman at Pearl Harbor?

"He found out about Art from a mutual friend," said Kathleen. "I saw him a few years later and he also had married."

Art Charboneau was always a big man, about 6-feet. A product of the Depression, he worked in a machine shop through high school and when he met Kathleen. He was also a fine baseball player. As a third baseman for an amateur hardball team, he was offered a $40-a-month contract by a scout for the St. Louis Cardinals. He was to play Class D baseball "somewhere in Missouri," recalled Art. "I turned it down because I was earning $12 a week in the plant." Later he served in the Navy for less than a year, released when his weight dropped 30 pounds, to 120, because of a lingering sickness he contracted while working in the machine shop. In 1945, Art Charboneau was told that his health required an outdoor job. That led to the seven years as a milkman and to the dwindling bank account as the couple's family increased.

After Art Jr. was born in December of 1943, Jim would arrive just 15 months later. Although Art Sr. was a convert, the Charboneaus were a good, productive Catholic family.

Joe Charboneau comes from interesting stock. Art Charboneau says that his ancestor came from France to Canada in the 1600s. Joe is a descendant of Toussaint Charbonneau, who along with his Indian princess wife, Sacagawea, led pioneers Lewis and Clark on the second leg of their expedition through the Northwest Territory.

Joe's great grandfather received a college education in New York. However, he did not enjoy the sedate life and became a trader on the high seas after school. For 24 years, he sailed to places like India and China.

"My father told me about my relatives," said Charboneau. "I understand that the French Charbonneau was this unsavory character who had a bunch of wives. I have French and Indian blood from my father and Dutch and Irish from my mother, which I guess would make me a mongrel."

Eventually, Kathleen Charboneau's prayers would be answered.

Art Charboneau discovered that he could make more money with his mouth than his back. He became a highly successful industrial salesman. But that was far from the end of the troubles for Kathleen Charboneau and her family.

THE AMERICAN DREAM, CALIFORNIA STYLE

Kathleen wanted her husband to be a success. She prayed for the better things in life for her family. As Art Charboneau found that he could talk his way into big deals which yielded even bigger dollars, all should have been well. Most marriages hit the rocks because of financial problems and the Charboneaus had finally overcome that hurdle.

But the price of an impressive bank account and bills marked "paid" was steep. Art Charboneau made his fortune on the road, and that meant weeks at a time away from home. It also meant that Kathleen Charboneau was in charge of six children, a task which often made her feel like a head zoo-keeper.

"Kathleen was very nervous at the time," said Art. "It would get worse. She felt a lot of pressure, first because of our financial problems and later because I was away so much. Part of the reason we made the move was that I thought it could help her and our marriage."

"The move" came in 1958. Art had been transferred from his job in Belvedere to Royal Oak, Michigan. Royal Oak is a suburb of Detroit with nearly 70,000 residents. There, the Charboneaus thought they had found the American Dream. They lived in a three-bedroom house on an acre lot with a pond in the back. Art and Kathleen had one bedroom, the four boys another, and the two girls slept in the third.

"Our house in Royal Oak was a great place," said Joe. "In our bedroom, all the beds were lined up. Since I was the youngest and the smallest, my brothers would throw me across the room from bed to bed. That was some experience because there were four beds."

Yes, life was good. There were two cars in the garage and a refrigerator bulging with food. The children had bikes and a slew of toys. Art Charboneau still seemed to be on the road for excruciatingly long periods, but he was a fine father when he was home. He played baseball with his sons and would watch 10-year-old Rick skate on their backyard pond as he practiced his hockey skills.

Royal Oak was also the site of Joe's first encounter with the opposite sex. He was five, and so was the girl, a neighbor named Kimberly. This "courtship" was more like Big Time wrestling than Romeo and Juliet.

"I wasn't really a bully," said Joe. "But I was always pushing Kimberly down, pulling her hair and ripping her new dresses. I'd put her on the swing in our back yard, knock her off and then put her back on. I think I got all this physical stuff from my brothers. They were always working me over because they wanted to make me tough. The amazing thing about Kimberly was that she kept coming back for more."

Kimberly's parents were not thrilled with their daughter's "friend." They were on good terms with the Charboneaus, and Kathleen had heard all the horror stories of the destroyed dresses, bumps and bruises inflicted by her son. As a last resort, Kimberly's parents forbade her to play with Joe, and so ended what will never be called a great American romance.

Joe and Kimberly would see each other once more, however. That day would remain etched in Joe's mind.

Art Charboneau continued to scale the business ladder and was offered several career opportunities in industrial sales. The most enticing came from a firm in Santa Clara, California.

"In Royal Oak, I had outgrown my position," said Art Charboneau. "I was making more money than the president of the company, and I needed a new challenge."

After five years in Royal Oak, the Charboneaus went west. Again, they seemed to be pursuing the American Dream. This time, they were headed to California. Meanwhile, Kimberly learned that Joe was leaving.

She had on a new dress and came over to say goodbye to me," said Joe. "I saw her coming. It was moving day. For some reason, I was too embarrassed to face her. I hid under the car. I think she saw me, but we never did say goodbye."

The trip west was made in two cars. Art Jr., the oldest child at 17, was behind the wheel of one automobile, and Art Sr. drove the other.

"We took a lot of time on the trip," said Joe. "It was summer, and we stopped along the way at a lot of the sights, like Mount Rushmore. I guess the trip was about 2,500 miles, and we made it in seven days."

In the early 1960s, California *was* the American Dream. It was the land of Hollywood, the sun and the blue Pacific. It was a place of self-made millionaires, and of losers looking for one more shot. The area received thousands of nicknames, most in the mold of "The Panacea by the Pacific." The state was growing by 10,000 weekly, its population having rocketed from 10,500,000 to 15,717,000 in the 1950s.

It was the summer of 1962 when Art Charboneau brought his family to Santa Clara. The San Francisco Bay community had a population of 60,000. There the Charboneaus moved into another comfortable home, and on the surface everything appeared idyllic. But that was an illusion, much like the California weather, which hides the underlying grit and poverty of the state.

Art and Kathleen were watching their marriage disintegrate. Art still spent more time away than in his own living room. His sales territory was the entire Pacific Northwest, and his trips were growing progressively longer. Despite Art Charboneau's ever-increasing income, which made life easier, Kathleen still fretted and worried, finding no relief for her nervous condition.

"The thing was that my parents never argued," said Joe. "I remember maybe one or two fights, and the subject was how to handle the children. My mother thought that Dad was being too strict. The only way I could detect that something was up was that my father was hardly ever around anymore. It got to the point where he would just show up for the holidays and then leave again."

A year after the move to California, Art and Kathleen separated. This was in 1963. They had just celebrated the birth of a fifth son, John, before the break. The couple's divorce would not be final until 1970, and Art Charboneau then remarried. He now lives in Glendale, a suburb of Phoenix, Arizona.

The departure of Art in 1963 turned the upper-middle-class family into one that had to scramble and scrounge to evade the grasp of poverty. The slide was gradual and steady. Joe Charboneau would live in four different houses and a dozen more apartments during his 16 years in California.

"We never were evicted or anything like that," said Joe. "But we would move into a place and find out that the rent had been raised or that we couldn't make the payments. So we would move some place cheaper. Each time we moved, it was to a lesser place."

It reached the point that picnic tables and benches served as furniture. Kathleen had sold most of the family's fine furnishing to pay the bills. Pictures, purchased at rummage sales for a dollar apiece, hung on the walls to cover the holes. The family car was a 1953 pink and black Chevy. Meat such as steak and beef was a luxury. If Joe did not eat everything on his plate, he could count on a frown and a stern lecture about frugality from his mother.

"Sometimes, I look back at those days and wonder how we made it," said Kathleen Charboneau. "It was tight, and we had only the necessities, but we got by. The kids stuck together and always pitched in. We are a very close family and always look out for each other. For example, Joe would not even let me go out to the store at night alone. He would go with me. He was always worried that someone might try to hurt me. We were very protective of each other."

Kathleen Charboneau is a proud and somewhat stubborn woman. She was determined to keep her family thriving despite the squalor which surrounded them. She refused welfare. She worked 12 to 14 hours a day as a receptionist at Kaiser Hospital. Times were harder than in her early years with Art Charboneau. Nevertheless, she would never criticize her husband or let her children do so. Nor would she ever date another man. Her faith was like steel which would never rust or break. She visited church daily and told her children that God would provide. She made more novenas and prayed for strength and guidance.

"My oldest sister Carol was like a mother to us," said Joe. "She cooked our meals and mended our clothes. Since Mom had to work, Carol ran the house. At this point, we only saw Dad at Christmas. I was very close to Carol and so was my mother. My mother would never say that anything was wrong, but at night I would hear her talking to Carol and sometimes crying. Carol sacrificed a lot to raise us. She had almost no social life. When she was in high school and a boy wanted to take her to the beach, she would say that she would have to bring along her younger brothers and sisters. Needless to say, that did not make her the most popular girl in school."

Kathleen and Carol spent hours each night making and mending clothes. They made sure that each of the children had at least one nice outfit for church, but Joe remembers that his mother would often glue her tattered shoes together.

"My mother wanted us to get a Catholic education," said Joe. "She paid extra to send us to St. Lawrence School. It was four miles from where we lived, and we would walk to school every day, leaving two hours before it started. I lasted at St. Lawrence until the seventh grade, when I was asked to leave because of my grades. By that time, all I wanted to do was to play baseball."

Baseball and the Charboneaus went together like politics and the Kennedys. Joe Charboneau was three the first time he tossed a baseball. The year was 1958. The Los Angeles Dodgers had just arrived from Brooklyn and were playing their first season on the West Coast. Their opener would attract 78,672 fans. Later that summer, Stan Musial was to register his 3,000th hit, a double off a pitcher named Moe Drabowsky. And in Royal Oak, Joe was playing catch with his older brother Rick.

"We bought the balls for 25 cents," said Joe. "They were filled with sawdust. You couldn't hit them or throw them against the wall. The cover was vinyl, and when they were hit they would explode into nothing but sawdust."

Three years later, Joe Charboneau was to obtain his first baseball glove. The year was 1961. Roger Maris was breaking Babe Ruth's single-season home run mark. A pitch delivered by Tracy Stallard was slammed by Maris for No. 61. Meanwhile, the Philadelphia Phillies were authoring a 23-game losing streak and 40-year-old pitcher Warren Spahn was winning his 300th game. And Joe Charboneau found that he was in love for the first time. The object of his affection was a vinyl baseball mitt. It had no pocket and a web which could barely contain a spider. But that hardly mattered. At six, your first glove is a precious jewel to be guarded and to always have in your possession. So what if Kathleen Charboneau had purchased it from the Thrifty Drug Store for only $6.

"Joe was so proud of that first glove," said Mrs. Charboneau. "He loved it. He would take it to bed at night and sleep with it under his pillow."

"I had that glove for years," said Joe. "It was held together by string and shoelaces when it finally deteriorated so badly that I had to get rid of it."

Bats were also a rare commodity.

"It was a long time before I had one of my own," said Joe. "Most of the time, I went out to diamonds and found some which had been broken, or ones where the knobs were crushed. I would take them home and nail and tape them up."

When Joe turned seven, he told his mother that he would like to play Little League baseball. The family had just moved to Santa Clara; Art Charboneau was seldom home. The year was 1962. In that year, Jackie Robinson became the first black to be elected to the Hall of Fame. Sandy Koufax struck out 18 Chicago Cubs. Bob Allison and Harmon Killebrew of the Minnesota Twins became the first players in Major League history to hit grand slams in the same inning. They did it in the Twins' 14-3 rout of the Cleveland Indians.

In Santa Clara, Kathleen Charboneau was walking two miles with her sons to sign them up for Little League baseball.

"I think I was more interested in their baseball than they were," said Mrs. Charboneau. "In our family, baseball was always tremendously important. It meant a lot to the boys and me. I was always worried about them missing their signup days and games. The first time I took Joe to Little League signups was at Scott Field in Santa Clara."

During their journey, Joe looked up at his mother and said, "Mom, some day I'm gong to be a big league ballplayer."

"That's fine," said Mrs. Charboneau.

"I'm serious," said Joe.

"I know you are," said Mrs. Charboneau. "You can do anything you want, if you are willing to work for it."

Joe Charboneau did not win Rookie of the Year honors in his initial Little League season. He began the year with a single up the middle and a 1.000 batting average. He would not bat again, and his average would remain perfect. Joe was not exactly a burgeoning star. He was cut from two Little League teams, mostly because of his size. He was dwarfed by his friends in the same age group, and this embarrassed him.

"I was not worried about the effects on Joe of his being cut," said Mrs. Charboneau. "He would never give up. He was very determined, and he wanted to play so badly. He would go out and play baseball all day with one bunch of kids, then find another bunch to play with until it got dark."

Because of the constant use, the vinyl baseball glove was falling apart. Besides, a prospective Major Leaguer does not make the big time with a vinyl glove.

Joe longed for a "real glove," one made of leather. The Charboneau family saved Blue Chip stamps. When the book was filled, Joe would have his dream. That day came in 1964. Cleveland Indians third baseman Max Alvis was struck with spinal meningitis. Los Angeles Angels pitcher Bo Belinsky was suspended for punching out a 64-year-old sportswriter. Yankee Manager Yogi Berra and utility player Phil Linz became involved in a raging argument over Linz's favorite activity of playing the harmonica on the team bus. And Joe finally received that leather mitt.

"The glove was too small," said Joe. "Carol went to the store and

picked out the wrong model. It was so small that I put my younger
brother John's name on it and told the rest of the kids that I had left
my regular glove at home and was using John's for a while. I used it
for half that season, and my coach kept calling me John."

It took more than three years for the then skinny Joe Charboneau
to hit his first home run. The kid had heard all the jokes about being
able to hide behind a flagpole or being thin enough to slip under a
door. But that never deterred him.

"Joe was so single-minded," said Mrs. Charboneau. "He would
work and work at something until he got it right. He usually played
with older kids. I remember one day I saw the group Joe was with
shinny up this pole in the schoolyard. Joe was only six at the time, and
he couldn't do it. For the next two weeks, he went to the schoolyard
every day and tried to go up the pole. Finally, he made it."

The year of the homer was 1965. Satchel Paige was 60, and he
pitched three innings for the Kansas City A's as they beat Boston, 5–2.
Frank Robinson was traded by the Cincinnati Reds to Baltimore for
Milt Pappas, Dick Simpson and Jack Baldschun. The smallest crowd
in Milwaukee history, 812, watched the Braves fall to Philadelphia,
4–1. And 10-year-old Joe Charboneau was at bat in a Santa Clara
Little League game. Taking a monstrous swing, Joe ripped a liner
between the center and left fielders. There was no fence, and the ball
seemed to roll for an eternity. By the time the ball was retrieved, Joe
had rounded all four bases.

"Our weekends used to revolve around baseball," said Mrs. Charboneau. "The five boys all played. We'd pack picnic lunches and go
from one game to another. It was our entertainment, and it was free.
All the boys loved baseball, but Joe was fanatical about it."

On the day of the home run, Joe was the only Charboneau present.

"He hit that first homer at Briarwood," said Mrs. Charboneau. "It
bothered him that no one from the family was there to see it. Things
like that really weighed on his mind. He wants to share everything."

One year later, Joe would add a pair of spikes to his wardrobe. The
year was 1966. The New York Mets signed 21-year-old Tom Seaver
out of the University of Southern California for a $50,000 bonus.
Sandy Koufax retired at age 29 because of an arthritic left arm which

required an inordinate number of pain-killing injections so that he could throw a baseball. The Milwaukee Braves moved to Atlanta.

At this point, money in the Charboneau household was scarce. Moths could have taken up residence in the kitchen cookie jar. Art Charboneau religiously sent support payments to his family, but there still was not enough to go around. Nevertheless, Joe Charboneau wanted spike shoes. He knew better than to ask his mother to buy them, so he became a minor entrepreneur.

"Joe caught frogs at a pond near our apartment," said Mrs. Charboneau. "He told everyone in the neighborhood that he had frogs for sale at 25 cents each. Kids were always knocking on our door wanting the frogs. I don't know what they did with them, but Joe had a good business going. One day, he came home with the spikes. But they were three sizes too big. I told him that he could fit both feet into one shoe. He wouldn't take them back. He said he would grow into them, and in the meantime he stuffed them full of tissue paper so he could wear them."

The plight of the family was registered in a picture of Joe in his Little League uniform. He was standing with the rest of the players, holding a hand over his left knee. His hand was hiding a hole in his baseball pants.

At 13, Joe's baseball career was stalled. The year was 1968. Montreal and San Diego were awarded National League franchises. Denny McLain won 31 games, leading the Detroit Tigers to a pennant. Catfish Hunter pitched a perfect game for the Oakland A's. Washington shortstop Ron Hansen pulled off an unassisted triple play against Cleveland. The batter was Joe Azcue. And on a baseball field in Santa Clara, Joe Charboneau tore up the ligaments in his right knee.

"I remember it as though it were yesterday," said Mrs. Charboneau. "He was sliding into second base. He not only tore up his knee, but he cut himself badly on some glass that had become mixed in with the dirt."

The knee began to swell and turn colors. It appeared that it would never stop hurting or growing in size. Eventually it did, and the doctors determined that it required a cast. For eight months, Joe

walked around dragging a casted leg. When the plaster came off, there
were four more months of rehabilitation. He winced and groaned
with every leg lift and squat. It seemed as though he would never have
full mobility of the knee.

"I always thought Joe would have chronic knee problems after
that," said Mrs. Charboneau. "It was very hard to keep him in the
cast; he wouldn't stay still. I heard that he went swimming with the
cast on and floated around the pool with his leg up in the air and out of
the water. When I found out about it, I set down some strict rules. But
that didn't stop him. I don't know how many times we had that cast
changed and repaired, but it seemed like it was happening all the time.
Once, he had to get his knee drained."

For two years, Joe Charboneau did not play baseball. Instead, he
found other ways to amuse himself, and none of them particularly
thrilled Mrs. Charboneau.

3 ★★★★★★

GROWING PAINS

Joe Charboneau grew up on the right side of the tracks, but just barely.

"I spent my early teens in this apartment right next to the railroad tracks," said Joe. "On the other side was a hobo camp and a settlement for migrant workers. Really, it was a ghetto. Around everything were miles and miles of trees, mostly plum, pear and apple. I remember looking down the tracks and seeing them lined with trees on both sides."

Between her job and the children, Kathleen Charboneau often lived in a frenzy. There was never enough time, money or room in their apartment. Inflation was eating away their income like a pack of termites going at a piece of wood. The family was moving at a rapid rate, always to a place with a lower rent.

"The apartment by the tracks was the worst place we had," said Joe. "It was totally run down. That is where we had nothing but picnic tables and benches for furniture. There were a lot of chances to get into trouble around there. The migrants were really wild."

When Joe looked out the window of his apartment, he could see the migrants' shacks.

"There were gangs everywhere," said Joe. "They all had their territory. It wasn't like the parts of New York City that are war zones, but it was rough. The members of the gangs carried knives and chains. There were places you simply couldn't walk. I was still small, and the gangs got off on beating me up. There would be no reason for it. They would come up to me and let the smallest kid in the gang beat the hell out of me. Usually it was a push and a kick, but it hurt. I couldn't do anything because the other members of the gang would jump me if I did."

Joe tried to hide the problems from his mother, but she was aware of the perils of the neighborhood. She desperately wanted to take the family elsewhere. A barren bank account dictated life by the tracks, however. Through her position at Kaiser Hospital, Kathleen Charboneau discovered that Joe was one of their frequent visitors. He usually showed up in the hospital emergency room, beaten and bloody. He was constantly being stitched, patched and reassembled after his various ventures with the local fruit pickers.

At 13, Joe was officially initiated into his neighborhood.

"I got into this fight with a Mexican kid," said Joe. "All of a sudden, the Mexican grabs a bottle, breaks it and sticks me in the arm. I went to the hospital, and I was bleeding. I told my mother that I cut it on a fence, but I don't think she believed me. The only person I would tell about the fights was my older sister Carol. I don't think she told my mother, but Mom always seemed to know what was happening."

One day, it seemed like Joe's neighborhood was hit by some type of plague. Men and teens sat in doorways and on the street sniffing and nodding. People walked about pushing pills to pedestrians.

"The drugs came all at once," said Joe. "Kids were sniffing glue and taking all kinds of pills. Older people were into the harder stuff. Probably only thirty to forty percent of the kids were doing drugs, but it seemed like everybody because they were so visible."

"I knew about the drugs, and I warned Joe and the rest of the kids about them," said Kathleen Charboneau. "I forbade the kids to go back to the shacks where the migrant workers lived. I knew they were getting into fights with the kids over there, but there wasn't much I could do about it because I was always working. I told them to leave if their friends started pulling out any drugs."

"I followed my mother's advice on drugs," said Joe. "She made them seem very dangerous and I never tried them. At 13, I did drink beer, though."

Joe also chewed tobacco and was tempted by a life of crime.

"A friend offered me $20 to steal this bike and give it to him," said Joe. "I took the bike, but then I got really worried. I was afraid the cops would get me, and then my mother would find out. So I returned it."

Charboneau also recalls breaking into a classroom and stealing candy from a teacher's desk, and a few other small incidents.

"I did like living by the tracks because there were a lot of places to play," said Joe. "Just down from our apartment was a creek and a bridge. I used to go swimming there and catch lizards. Also, close to the tracks was an onion field right near the hobo camp. There was an abandoned farmhouse, and we used to explore it. My mother told me not to do that stuff, but I did anyway."

Lizards consumed much of his time. Joe and his friends would each catch eight to ten and then put them in someone's front lawn. The grass would be a choppy sea of leaping lizards.

"The other thing that was fun was to put a penny or small rock on the tracks and watch the trains run over it," said Joe. "They say that is dangerous, but nothing ever happened. We also would hide in the woods and throw pears at the trains when they came by. The train detectives would come out and chase us, but they were big fat guys, and it wasn't very hard to lose them in the orchards."

There was one very close call with a train, however.

"A bunch of us were playing by the tracks," said Joe. "We heard a train coming and were trying to beat it across the double tracks. When my turn came, the train seemed awful close. It was bearing down on me, but I took off anyway. I thought I made it by 20 feet, but all my friends looked really scared. They thought I was smashed for sure."

Needless to say, Joe was never to be confused with an excellent student. While his sister Carol brought home straight As, Joe spent more time in the principal's office than in the classroom. He thought books were there to be thrown at people. He was asked to leave St. Lawrence School in the seventh grade because of his poor academic performance. In high school, he would need tutors to keep him eligible for athletics.

"Joe had concentration problems," said Kathleen Charboneau. "He is an intelligent person with an above-average IQ. I talked to a lot of his teachers, and they said he could not sit still. Joe is a very physical person, and he has so much energy. He can't stay in one place for very long."

"I was cutting a lot of classes, my grades were lousy and I was generally wild," admitted Joe.

It became evident that Joe needed a large dose of discipline. He was stepping dangerously close to the line of what was defined as socially acceptable behavior. Kathleen Charboneau did not know what to do about his poor grades and endless fights.

"I felt Joe needed a father," said Kathleen Charboneau. "Joe's dad had been a strong disciplinarian. I called him in Portland and asked him to take care of Joe for a while. I was losing my grip on him. In California, he was faced with so many problems. I thought this would be the best thing to do. Five boys make you tired, and I felt that Joe's father would be a big help to him."

In Portland, Joe moved in with his father, a stepmother and two stepbrothers.

"It was really weird," said Joe. "I couldn't get used to my father being married to another woman. At first I didn't get along with my stepmother."

Charboneau had ambivalent feelings toward his father. He liked and respected the man, but he was hurt when his parents separated.

"As a kid, I felt cheated because other kids had a father at home all the time and I didn't. I always thought that if my father was there, I would be able to go camping and have more things like we had in Royal Oak. Thoughts like that ran through my mind."

In reality, Art Charboneau did not completely abandon his family, as some magazine and newspaper articles have suggested.

"I always made the support payments and visited the kids on Christmas," said Art Charboneau. "I had three of the kids living with me in Portland at various times. Two of my sons, Jim and Art, eventually settled in Portland, so I could not have been such a bad guy. I helped Kathleen with the kids whenever she asked. The fact is that a divorce is never easy for anyone involved."

While Art still earned his living in sales, he also owned a fishing boat.

"Joe loved the boat," said Art. "We would go on long trips fishing for salmon. We had talks on the boat about life and what Joe was doing with himself. I told him that he had to shape up. He should stick to school and sports and stay away from that other stuff. When he came to me, Kathleen couldn't handle him any more, and he had also been in some scrapes. In Portland, he settled down and got his priorities straight."

Art Charboneau is a tall man with broad shoulders and a lined, rugged face. Like Joe, he has a fondness for cowboy hats. He also has the type of authoritative voice which forces one to listen. When he walks into a room, all eyes seem to swing in his direction. He has a presence, a kind of charisma, which cannot be ignored.

Fully recovered from his knee injury, Joe took his father's advice and returned to baseball. As a high school freshman, he was the MVP of the Park Rose Heights baseball team. He hit his first home run since Little League and saw himself mature. He went to Portland at 5'2", weighing 100 pounds. A year later, he returned to his mother in Santa Clara at 5'10", and 150 pounds. Keeping him in clothes was an impossibility.

"Portland was good for me," said Joe. "My dad put my head on straight. I was back playing baseball and doing better than I ever had. My brother also got me interested in lifting weights. I love weights. But I missed my mother from the day I left, and every day I wanted to go home. It has always been very hard for me to be apart from her."

"Sending Joe to Portland was an ordeal," said Kathleen Charboneau. "I missed him so much. We were calling back and forth all the time. If anything, we became closer than we had been. Going to Portland didn't hurt him. He had a good time and made some friends, but I don't know if I would do it again."

Joe's reunion with his mother was a powerful and touching scene. There has always been a strong, almost metaphysical, bond between the two. It began with the unusual circumstances of his birth. In his first year, Kathleen Charboneau constantly had the child in her arms.

"After he came back, I think Joe was very afraid that we might be permanently separated," said Kathleen Charboneau. "I would be watching television, and he would lie down on the floor right beside me. He was like a little puppy, always following me around. He wouldn't let me go anywhere alone."

It was 1971 when Joe left Portland for Santa Clara. Nine years later, he would still feel that close relationship with his mother. On Thanksgiving Day, 1980, Joe was in Cleveland while his mother remained in California. It was the first time they had ever been apart on this holiday. Joe telephoned her four times to tell her how much he missed her.

BUMPS AND BRUISES

While Joe claimed to have been changed by his stay in Portland, his actions upon his return to Santa Clara showed that there was little different about him. In school, he again wrestled with the books and was pinned, this time being ruled ineligible for athletics during his sophomore year of high school.

But he graduated to a new form of frolic by the railroad tracks. Actually, school could be blamed for Charboneau's latest antics.

"In English class, they had us read this book called *The Learning Tree*," explained Joe. "It was about these kids who would all go into this ring and push and fight until one emerged as a winner."

Instead of a ring, Joe used a boxcar.

"We would get 25 guys, and each would throw a buck into a hat," said Joe. "Then we would climb into a flatbed or boxcar. We would start pushing and shoving until there was only one guy left. He would get the money. It was a lot like king of the hill. Toward the end, it got pretty rough. Guys were punching each other, and we got worried that somebody might be pushed out of the car and bust his head on the tracks. The funny thing was that I thought up the game, but I never won any money."

It was a natural step from this activity to his next endeavor.

Around Santa Clara, there was a rumor of boxing matches held in boxcars. Word was that you could put up $5 and come home with $20 or $25, if you were strong and tough enough to punch out your opponent without the benefit of gloves. Those money figures impressed Joe, whose wardrobe carried the Salvation Army label.

Joe had come back from Portland with a bigger and better build than he had taken with him. Between weight-lifting and the natural growing process, he had turned his once fragile frame into one with rock-hard muscles. Also, he now felt that he could match anyone who wanted a brawl. Bare-fisted fighting intrigued Joe. He had watched the televised boxing matches in the late 1960s and early 1970s.

"I figured I could do what those guys on TV were doing," said Joe. "I wanted to prove something to myself. I remembered all the times those gangs beat the hell out of me when I was a kid. I wanted to show everyone that I was tough enough to fight back, and that I wasn't going to take anything from anybody."

There is nothing new about bare-fisted fighting. It can be traced back to 1816 in the United States when a couple of pugilists named Tom Beasley and Jacob Hyer slugged it out in New York City.

In Santa Clara, bare-fisted brawling is illegal, but that fact did not faze the local folks who ran the operation. Like the local cockfights, bare-fisted boxing was ignored by the Santa Clara police, who were paid well for looking the other way.

The fights were organized by "some guys who wore black suits and drove huge Cadillacs," according to Joe. "I always thought that they were with the Mafia, but I never knew for sure. All I know is that they told me never to worry about the cops or the railroad detectives, because they had been taken care of. The other thing was that the location of the fights would change from time to time to keep the heat off."

Friday and Saturday evenings were fight nights by the Santa Clara tracks. Between the orchards and the migrant shanties, one of the most gruesome activities ever conceived by men would be played out before fruit pickers, who smelled of whiskey or cheap wine and who bet what little income they made from their subsistence jobs.

"They would put us in boxcars and match us up according to our ability," said Joe. "They didn't want some inexperienced kid getting killed by some guy who had been doing that kind of thing for ten years. Some of the fights featured older fat guys who were the regulars. The winner would get around $200 in those fights and guys would bet $50 to $100, and more, on the outcome.

"There were no rules," continued Joe. "You could bite, push, shove, punch or do anything else. It was amazing how brutal guys would be. They would kick, butt heads, anything went. Anywhere from twenty to fifty guys would watch you fight. I always was in the lesser matches, and no one bet more than $5 on my fights."

In his rookie fight, Joe immediately learned that this was not exactly what the Marquis of Queensberry had in mind when he drew up what he considered the proper etiquette for boxing. The boxcar was almost dark inside. Holes had been cut in the roof of the car to let in some light from a lamp post near the tracks. The place reeked of booze and blood. His opponent was a frail Mexican. Like Joe, he had had no previous boxcar brawling experience. Both fighters stripped off their shirts.

"I hit the kid once," said Joe. "Then he got me. I mean he really cleaned my clock."

Bloodied, bruised and battered, Joe limped off. He was booed, kicked, spat upon and slapped by those who had bet on him.

"When you lost, you didn't stay around very long because the guys who lost money on you would get you," said Joe. "Usually, the winner in fights like mine made thirty bucks and the loser got twenty. The fight promoters got five."

The initial beating did not deter Joe. The possibility of earning a few bucks and the physical aspects of the event drew him like a magnet.

"In my second fight, I got my nose broken," said Joe. "I have my mother's nose. She can break it just by touching it against a door."

The actual bouts did not last long. Two or three minutes and a winner would emerge. It was not uncommon for the loser to lie in a heap, shaking and vomiting. Some of the participants were flabby middle-aged men looking for a few extra dollars. Sometimes, they would succumb in 30 seconds because of exhaustion.

"There was nothing pretty about it," said Joe. "It was just a brawl."

Charboneau did not want his mother to discover his latest sideline. One day, he wiped his bloody nose with his shirt. Realizing his mistake, he decided to hide the shirt deep in his closet. His mother found it and confronted him with it.

"He told me he had been fighting," said Kathleen Charboneau. "That sort of thing always worried me. At the time, I didn't know the circumstances of the fights. I knew that he didn't go around picking fights with anyone, but that he wouldn't back down if he was challenged. I felt this was all a part of his growing up."

Joe did not even want his friends to know about his boxcar fighting. He felt somewhat embarrassed talking about it, but he was also uplifted by the knowledge that he was tough enough to handle himself in that type of setting. He says he engaged in about 40 fights during his two-year career and emerged as a winner about half of the time. His earnings from all of this were no more than $300. He seldom made more than $20 from a fight, and he was lucky if 30 people watched this form of insanity.

"I reached the point where I got sick of hitting people," said Joe. "I was always worried about getting caught by the cops, and I would get out of there fast after the fights. Everybody got fat lips and black eyes. I developed bone chips in my right elbow, and my nose was broken at least three times."

Years later, Joe would still be haunted by his pugilist days. His already crooked teeth grew at even more bizarre angles. His nose was a disaster area, and there were slivers in his arms from hitting the walls and floors of the decaying wooden boxcars. All this for $300.

The one incident which convinced Joe that the end was near occurred in a fight he won.

"I knocked out this guy with one punch," said Joe. "At first, I felt real good about it. Everybody was patting me on the back, saying that I was great. Then I thought about it for a moment, and I realized that I could have killed the guy. Thinking about it made me sick and scared. Another time, I saw a guy get knocked out of the car, and he smashed his head on the ground. He just barely survived. It made me wonder if it was worth it. It seemed like you lost every time you fought because of the beating you took."

During the 1980 baseball season, Joe would meet fans who had read of his boxcar escapades.

"These guys told me that they still fight in cars on the New York waterfront," said Joe. "I hear it goes on elsewhere, too. It is a lot like the strongman competition they have going on these days."

Joe's final fight was during the summer between his junior and senior years in high school. He never had the urge to fight again until he read about professional football player Ed "Too Tall" Jones retiring from the Dallas Cowboys to take a crack at the heavyweight boxing title.

"But when I saw how foolish 'Too Tall' looked in the ring on TV, I forgot about trying boxing myself," said Joe.

There is more to Joe Charboneau than bare-fisted boxing and baseball. In fact, that was the conservative side of Joe. During his years at Buchser High, his eccentricities were rivaled by none.

One day he was watching television with a friend. On the screen a snake slithered up to an egg and swallowed it whole: One mighty gulp—and it was gone.

"I can do that," Joe said to his friend.

"Get out of here," said the friend. "No way."

"Watch," said Joe.

Undaunted, Joe walked to the refrigerator and pulled out an egg, a hardboiled egg.

"No snake will outdo me," Joe said with an odd smile. He opened his mouth so wide that he thought his lips would rip. Then he shoved the egg in and swallowed. Slowly, the egg made its way down. But there was a problem.

"I got it halfway down my throat when it got stuck," said Joe. "I started turning purple. Finally, I motioned for my friend to hit me on the back."

Joe's pal whacked him. The egg shell broke, and down it went.

"I never tried that one again," said Joe.

It didn't matter. Joe had plenty of other stunts to occupy his time. On another occasion, Joe and a friend named Horatio were walking home from school when they spotted several cherry trees in a farmer's orchard. The cherries looked ripe and red, good and ready to be picked and eaten. But there was a problem. A barbed-wire fence surrounded the orchard.

Not about to be discouraged by this interesting challenge, Joe and Horatio carefully worked their way through the fence. In doing so, Joe cut his arm above the right elbow. Suddenly, there was blood everywhere. The wound was gushing. Joe grabbed the gash with his free hand, and they dashed to his house. No one was home.

"What are we going to do?" asked Horatio.

"Listen, we'll just sew it up," said Joe.

"You're kidding."

"I've been sewed up by doctors enough to know what to do. What else are we supposed to do?" asked Joe.

Charboneau found a needle and some fishing line. He was about to start the operation when he stopped.

"Hey, sterilize the needle," Joe said, handing it to Horatio.

Horatio dropped the needle into boiling water and then pulled it out, pronouncing it clean. Then he watched in horror as Joe took the needle and line and began stitching his own wound: in and out; in and out; once more, in and out.

"No more," said Horatio. "I can't watch any more of this."

Neither could Joe. The three stitches had closed the wound. They were removed a few hours later, but the grotesque scars from this crude piece of medical procedure can be shown to you by Joe today. Obviously, Charboneau had little aversion to blood, and he proved it by the famed tattoo incident.

In the 1970s, tattoos were the rage of Buchser High. Kids were slapping dragons, hearts, monsters and naked women on their arms and legs, with the help of needles and India ink. Naturally, Joe was in the middle of this craze. He had punched out a face tattoo on one of his arms. He added his initials to the inside of his right hand.

Like Hula Hoops and Edsels, the tattoo fad ran its course. Unlike a

Hula Hoop, which can be tossed in the garbage, or an Edsel that can be junked, tattoos stay on your skin.

"My sister told me that I had to get rid of those things," said Joe. "She said my mother hated them."

Charboneau took the painful route. He scraped them off with a razor blade.

"It really hurt," said Joe. "But I never got infected. It is amazing that I never got an infection from any of that stuff. I think it was because I got my tetanus shots regularly."

Tetanus shots weren't the only shots Charboneau was taking during this period.

One day he and a pal of his, bored with it all, decided they wanted to practice some archery. The bow and arrows belonged to the friend's dad, who used them for hunting. The pair of would-be hunters took the bow and several arrows and went out to shoot. They set up a target, and Charboneau's pal took the first turn. Joe was standing 15 feet from his buddy when, suddenly, he was struck in the stomach with a wayward arrow.

"I couldn't believe it," said Joe. "The arrow wasn't coming hard enough to stick, but it caused an indentation and some blood. To this day, I think he was shooting at me on purpose."

A scar from being grazed by an arrow remains on the right side of Joe Charboneau's stomach.

This stomach has taken other punishment. Joe once ate half-a-dozen cigarettes on a dare. They were the filter-tip variety, no less. "I held them down for about two minutes," he said. "Then I threw them up." He collected $5 for that trick.

When challenged to do something fantastic or odd, Joe would almost always respond by attempting it. One classmate approached Joe with an interesting bet.

"I saw a guy eat glass on television," the friend told Joe.

"Nah," said Joe.

"He ate a shot glass. I saw him," insisted the friend. "I bet you can't do it."

Never one to back off, Charboneau tried it. Chewing vigorously for a minute or so, Joe finally gave up when his mouth began bleeding profusely.

"It wasn't exactly the smartest thing I've ever done," admitted Joe. "And I still don't think anyone can eat glass."

From the time he began fighting in the boxcars, Joe's nose took a regular beating. It was pushed from one side of his face to the other. Joe finally grew weary of hospitals.

Once, after falling out of a tree and breaking his nose, he decided to pass up yet one more hospital trip. Finding a vise grip and some cotton, he set the break himself.

"It wasn't bad," Joe said. "It didn't take long for the nose to straighten out."

Joe's predicaments often extended into the animal kingdom. During his sophomore year in high school, Joe and his sister Mary spent an afternoon horseback riding. The horse Joe rode did not particularly take to its rider. It continually turned its head trying to bite his leg. Later in the day when Joe had dismounted, and as he was helping Mary do the same, his horse finally accomplished what he had been trying so long to do. He bit his rider.

"He got me in the back," said Joe, who still carries the mark.

"I would hear about a lot of the things that happened to him, and I'd find them hard to believe," said Kathleen Charboneau. "I also remember one morning he woke up and his upper lip was swollen all out of shape. He looked like one of the Addams family, really like a monster. We took him to the doctor and found out that he had been bitten by a spider during the night. The wound eventually broke open and drained, after we had sent him to the infectious disease clinic."

Between bites and gashes, Joe did manage to play some baseball.

5 ★ ★ ★ ★ ★ ★ ★

COLLEGE

Until the last two weeks of high school, Joe was not aware that Major League baseball held an amateur-free-agent draft. He thought that players just signed with big league teams. There was supposedly nothing formal or complicated about it. A scout saw you play, was impressed and then offered you a contract. Indeed, that was the system until the 1960s. Now, all Major League clubs engage in a selection process. The pool includes all of the amateur players who have completed their high school education or college players who have turned 21. Scouts supply their teams with the list of athletes they consider professional material. Teams draft according to their won-lost record. The worst team picks first, followed by the team with the second worst record, and so on with the winningest club choosing last.

"I remember the final few days of high school," said Joe. "I was really depressed because two guys on my team got drafted and I didn't. I remember the last day of school. We had a game and a party afterwards. I refused to take my baseball uniform off. I wore it to the party, but I didn't stay long because I was upset about not getting picked. I also remember that I got kind of drunk and went home and slept in my uniform."

There was little reason for scouts to be excited about Joe. He batted

ninth in his junior year and was the leadoff man as a senior. His forte
was hitting singles and stealing bases.

"As a senior I probably batted about .330," said Joe. "But we had
guys on our team hitting .500 and more. I can look back now and see
that I wasn't anything great."

Joe played for Buchser High, a strong school in the Bay area. In his
senior year, his team was beaten for the Santa Clara city championship by a pitcher named Sandy Wihtol. Wihtol would later be a
teammate of Charboneau's with the Indians, and he still kids Joe
about his strikeouts in that final game.

But there was one scout who was interested in Charboneau. His
name was Eddie Bockman. Bockman is a little man, about 5-foot-5,
with a red face and a head that is thick with white hair. "He always
reminded me of Santa Claus," said Joe.

Bockman works for the Philadelphia Phillies, and his turf is the Bay
area. Most baseball fans have not heard of Eddie Bockman, and that
is a shame. If there were a Hall of Fame for scouts, Bockman would be
enshrined. In their lifetimes, most scouts are pleased if two of the
players they sign eventually play in the Majors. Ten of Bockman's
athletes have made it, and five have been in All-Star games. Larry
Bowa, Bob Boone, Randy Lerch, Warren Brusstar and John Vuko-
vich are among the players signed by Bockman.

"I first saw Joe play when he was a junior," said Bockman. "I went
to watch another player on Joe's team. That player was Steve Bart-
kowski, who is now the Atlanta Falcons quarterback. In that game,
Joe hit this monster homer. It had to be well over 400 feet. When you
see a junior hit a ball that far, it makes any scout sit up and take
notice."

"The funny thing about that home run is that it was the only one I
hit in high school," said Joe. "I was very lucky that Eddie Bockman
was there to see it."

Following the homer, Bockman returned to scout Charboneau. "I
must have watched him five or six times that year, and he never did a
thing," said Bockman. "But there was something about that home
run, and something about Joe which made me think he was special."

While Bockman liked Charboneau, he knew that Joe was not prepared for professional ball after high school.

Bockman is an old-style scout. His method is to become acquainted with everything about a player—his family, his personality, his performance at school and at work.

"You could tell that Joe was looking for a father," said Bockman. "He would confide in me, and never mentioned his own father. I got to know his family, his girlfriend, and I was at his wedding. In the process, I got to know what was in his heart, and a player must have a good heart, an attitude that will enable him to handle adversity, if he is going to make it in the pros."

In a sense, Bockman is an anachronism. Today's scouts work with computer printouts, issued by the Major League Scouting Bureau. Most do not bother to watch a marginal prospect like 17-year-old Joe Charboneau more than once. You can count on one hand the number of scouts who would take the trouble Bockman did with Joe.

"After I got out of high school, Eddie Bockman let me play for his summer team," said Joe. "He was that kind of guy. Here he was a scout, and in his spare time he managed a summer team for kids. He was sort of a local legend because he signed guys like Larry Bowa, who no one else thought could play. And they became stars. I remember that every Friday he would take me out to this high school, and he would throw batting practice to me and help me with my outfield defense. The best thing I can say about Eddie Bockman was that he was a father to me."

"I had heard about the fighting and some of the other crazy stunts Joe pulled, but what I liked about Joe was that he loved to work," said Bockman. "He worked hard for everything he got. He really pushed himself to become a good player. He looked out for his mother, too."

Starting with his junior year of high school, Charboneau placed himself on a grueling daily program. He lifted weights. He swung a lead bat 200 times a day. He hit a baseball off a tee 100 times. Eventually, all this would pay off.

Charboneau spent that summer after high school playing for Eddie Bockman and working at the TOYS-R-US store. During the summer, a scout from the Detroit Tigers expressed a token interest in Joe, but he never heard from the man again.

"I was kind of lost that summer," said Joe. "I had no decent job offers, no scholarships and no chance to play pro ball. My mother and I talked it over and we decided that I should go to school."

Joe enrolled at West Valley Junior College. The Saratoga, California, school was near Joe's home, and he was able to attend tuition-free because it was a state institution available to all California residents. His only bill was $50 each semester for books.

In high school, Joe was not exactly a scholar. His mother calls him "an average student," which is a nice way of saying that he never punched the principal and stayed out of trouble long enough to receive a diploma.

"I kept my job at the toy store and decided that I would go out for the baseball team at West Valley," said Joe. "The school had a good baseball reputation, and I thought that maybe I could catch somebody's attention there."

West Valley's coach was a man named Steve Bordi. He had played in the Kansas City Royals Minor League system.

"They had a fall baseball team, and I don't think Bordi knew who I was when I went out," said Joe. "Certainly no one was thrilled to see me try out for the team. I remember that we had forty guys hustling for the outfield positions and about a hundred went out for the team. I was overshadowed, and I think I was on the verge of getting cut, when a few players quit."

Joe's freshman year was not very notable. He batted only .240, but showed some power.

In January, the Major League clubs hold a draft for players in junior college, or those who had been drafted before but had decided not to sign. Charboneau was selected by the Minnesota Twins in the sixth round. There were 147 players picked in front of him, which meant that the Twins were not overwhelmed by him. In fact, his selection almost seemed like an afterthought on their part.

"Lee Irwin was the Twins' scout in my area, and he saw me play for Eddie Bockman's winter team," said Joe. "After the Twins picked me, he called me up and said he would come over to my house and take me out to dinner. Then we would talk about my future with the Twins."

Irwin arrived at Joe's home. Joe found out that there would be no dinner. Irwin had a contract in his hand and wanted to make a quick agreement with Joe and Mrs. Charboneau. He showed the document to Joe. It called for a $500 bonus. Joe was obviously quite disappointed with the extremely small bonus, and refused to sign the contract. Joe had certainly been hoping to receive a substantial bonus, since the thing he wanted most was to buy his mother a house. When Joe expressed his desires, a heated discussion ensued.

"You have got to be kidding," said Irwin. "You are lucky to be drafted. No other teams appeared to be interested in you, so I figured I'd draft you and give you a chance. I thought we could get you for a small bonus.

"Listen, son," continued Irwin. "If you are smart, you will sign this. As a player, you have a lot of weaknesses. You can't pull the ball, and you can't throw. You are a fringe prospect at best."

At this point, Joe's eyes were filled with tears. This was to be his dream moment. A big league scout was coming with a ticket to play baseball for a living, and this man had the gall to say the only reason he wanted Joe was because he thought he could sign him for little money.

"Mr. Irwin, if you feel that way about Joe, I think you should leave our house," said Mrs. Charboneau.

"Listen, Ma'am, I am just telling you how it is."

"I suggest that you leave," she repeated. Joe then stood up. His fists were clenched. He wanted to slug Irwin. Instead, he showed the scout to the door.

"What bothered me the most was that he had the contract filled out in advance," said Joe. "I was sure that if I signed for $500, the Twins would look at me for a few games and then let me go. They would have nothing invested in me, so they wouldn't give me a good shot. I had seen it happen to other guys. The big thing I couldn't figure out was that he had drafted me and had a contract in his hand, but he kept telling me that I couldn't play."

Later, Joe would receive a letter of apology from Irwin and the Twins. The bonus had been raised to $1,200, but Joe had decided that he never wanted to be associated with Minnesota again.

Charbonneau's sophomore year would be a memorable one. It would be the year he would blossom on the field. It was also the year he would meet Cindy Engle at a Fourth of July party. Cindy Engle would eventually become Mrs. Joe Charboneau.

Like Joe, Cindy went to Buchser High, but she is three years younger.

"I don't think Joe knew I existed while he was in high school," said Cindy. "He had this reputation as a tough guy, and I had heard that he had done some wild things. He was like the top gun in town, and all the other guys who thought they were tough would come up and challenge him to a fight."

Cindy also knew of Joe's relationships with women.

"I heard he had been through a few girls," said Cindy. "In high school, he was one of the big jocks, so it was no surprise that he had a few girlfriends."

Joe and Cindy were invited to a Fourth of July party at the house of a mutual friend. Both were going with other people at the time.

"I remember seeing Cindy across the room," said Joe. "She had blond hair down to the middle of her back. That's the first thing I noticed about her."

To Joe, Cindy Engle looked like one of those fabled California Golden Girls. She was 5-foot-8 with a swimmer's long and sleek body. He was infatuated with her before they ever spoke.

"I saw Joe across the room looking at me," said Cindy. "He was more than a little into his beer. He just kept smiling at me. I had a boyfriend at the time, and I didn't think much of Joe. I sort of ignored him."

Joe would not be dissuaded by Cindy's lack of interest. He walked over to her. Cradling a beer can in both hands, he sat down on a counter nearby. He started talking. The conversation was not memorable, but there was something about Joe's smile which finally enticed Cindy.

"I probably wouldn't have gone up to Cindy if I hadn't been drinking," said Joe. "Really, I am very shy with women."

Following their meeting over the counter, all was quiet for a week.

"I didn't expect to hear from him, because he was going to be a sophomore in college and I was just a junior in high school," said Cindy. "Then I got a phone call from my girlfriend, who also knew Joe. She said that Joe wanted to take me out. She said that Joe thought I might not remember who he was, but I had a very clear picture of him. I figured I might as well go out with him and see what happened."

That first date was an episode out of "Happy Days." Cindy heard Joe coming a mile away. A car with no muffler has its own way of announcing its arrival by making sounds like a moose with an upset stomach.

"I loved that car," said Joe. "It was three years old when I bought it, and it cost me $2,000. It was my first car, and I saved up for it by working at TOYS-R-US."

Cindy and Joe often talk of that car and the first date. The car was a 1972 Javelin. Its rear end was jacked up and its nose pointed toward the ground. There were mag-wheels and tires a foot wide. The seats were soft and deep, out of the old bucket mold. The Javelin had yellow and black racing stripes.

Joe wanted to impress his new girl. He took her to a very expensive restaurant named Bellows and then to a movie.

"I remember that we talked for 15 minutes and that was it," said Joe. "I had said everything I could, and Cindy wasn't saying anything. Her being so quiet sort of bothered me, but it was also kind of nice, because my previous girlfriends never knew when to shut up."

"The thing I remember most about that first date was that this tough guy did not know what to say," said Cindy. "But I kind of liked him, too."

A few more dates followed, and soon Cindy Engle and Joe Charboneau were a pair. They would go out for a hamburger and a movie. Then they would sit in that yellow-and-black-striped Javelin in front of Cindy's house for more than an hour.

"We weren't old enough to go to a bar and talk after a movie, so we

sat in front of her house," said Joe. "Later, as we got to know each
other better, we would go up to the mountains."

The relationship grew, and Joe learned the story of Cindy Engle.

Like Joe, Cindy was raised in a broken home. Her parents were
divorced when she was four. Her father then worked for the Park
Service at Crater Lake. He lived in a log cabin. Cindy's mother,
Margaret, remained in San Jose, and like Kathleen Charboneau, had
not remarried. She supported Cindy and her sister Mary from her
salary as a bookkeeper.

At eight, Cindy became interested in swimming. Her specialty was
synchronized swimming. She would train three hours in the morning
and three more hours at night. By the time she was a teenager, she was
ranked No. 1 in her age group. Cindy was also a member of the Santa
Clara Aquamaids. Swimming took her to Germany, Sweden, Switz-
erland and across the United States, as she competed with a team
called the California Coralettes.

Soon Cindy and Joe were going steady. She was doing his homework and listening to his woes and dreams.

"I've been very lucky," said Joe. "In high school, my girlfriend did
my homework, and in college Cindy did it. I don't think I ever did any
homework."

Joe's sophomore season was a product of those years of sweating
with weights and the lead bat. It was the culmination of everything
every baseball coach had ever told him. Finally, it was the justification
for all the time Eddie Bockman had spent with that kid from Santa
Clara.

In that season at West Valley, Joe wore his hair in a marine cut,
because that is how his coach thought a baseball player should look.
He played the game in a rage, with determination that was almost
frightening at times. He dove for balls, knocked pivoting second
basemen on their butts, and sometimes swung so hard that his batting
helmet flew off as he fell down going after a pitch.

But most of all, he began to hit like never before. His line drives
were sharp and crisp. They sounded like gunshots. His fly balls got up
in the air and carried as if they were aided by some jet stream. He was

still his team's leadoff batter, but he led his conference with 12 homers. He batted .373 and stole 14 bases.

Now, Eddie Bockman was just one of several scouts at his games, but Joe had his heart set on playing for the Phillies.

"Eddie Bockman had been so good to me," said Joe. "He worked so hard and really made me into a good player. I prayed that the Phillies would draft me."

Bockman went to Joe's last junior college contest and watched his protégé go 4-for-5 with two homers. "It was only then that Joe was really ready for pro ball," said Bockman. "He had matured both physically and mentally. I recommended that the Phillies take him."

Philadelphia selected Joe in the second round of the secondary phase of the June 1976 draft. Bockman came over to Joe's house with a contract calling for a $5,000 bonus. He would also receive another $1,000 if he played Class A for 90 days. If he lasted three months in Class AA, $1,500 more would come his way. He would receive another $3,500 for making Class AAA, and $5,000 more for playing in the Majors. In all, the package was worth $16,000 if Joe were to be on a Major League roster for 90 days.

"Everybody was thrilled for Joe," said Cindy. "His mother was overjoyed, and so was my mom. Joe and my mother got along great. He used to come over to our house and do chores for us. But when he left for the Minors I still didn't think we would get married."

"I took my bonus money and bought a 1973 VW Superbeetle," said Joe. "We needed a car because I had been unable to keep up the payments on my Javelin and had to sell it."

The Minors

6 ★★★★★★

SPARTANBURG

After settling upon a bonus with Eddie Bockman, Joe was told that the Phillies would pay him a $500-a-month salary only during the four months of the baseball season. They were sending him to play for their New York–Pennsylvania Class A Rookie League club in Auburn, New York.

On June 12, 1976, Joe flew to Auburn to begin his professional career, leaving the new Volkswagen with his mother.

"I don't remember very much about Auburn," said Joe. "I was there for only eight days. The season had not started, and I just worked out. I did celebrate my twenty-first birthday there on June 17. I was really looking forward to it, because it meant that I could go to bars now. But in New York, it was no big deal because the legal drinking age there is 18."

Most of the players on rookie league clubs are straight out of high school. For this reason, Philadelphia changed its mind about Joe and decided that he should go to Spartanburg, South Carolina, and play for the Phillies' Class A Western Carolina League club.

"Spartanburg was considered a more advanced club than Auburn," said Joe. "They had more players of college age. The strange thing was that they kept me in Auburn working out until one day before the season opened."

After this stutter step, Charboneau's career finally began.

For anyone who grew up in the San Francisco Bay Area, where cool breezes and green, mountainous scenery abound, the switch to Spartanburg is a culture shock. The place is hot, brown and flat. It is the typical aging Southern town. People are provincial, speak in slow drawls and are very skeptical of those who don't. Walking down the street on a July afternoon is enough to cause a deluge of sweat. It is a town of Anglicans and strict Baptists, debutante balls, and front porches where people sip lemonade and mint juleps. It is also a place where rural blacks live in houses with no doors, electricity or running water. In the back are outhouses with Sears catalogs available for toilet paper. Those South Carolina neighborhoods are in a time-warp.

To this place the Phillies shipped ballplayers from across the nation. Here they began to pursue the Major League brass ring. For many, it was their first time away from home, and that in itself was a trauma. Most of them had been the stars of their high school or college teams. Suddenly, they all seemed to be either struggling or of just average talent. It was quite a blow to their egos, and they either recovered and made it or they were let go.

On his first day at Spartanburg, Joe came to the realization that baseball would never be quite the same. Spartanburg pitcher Dickie Noles had just been knocked out of the box. He was banging things around the locker room, screaming and berating some of his teammates.

"Hey, take it easy," said Joe.

"Who are you?" Noles asked Joe. "What do you know about it? You open your mouth one more time to me, and I'm gonna break your jaw."

Charboneau saw the crazed look in Noles's eyes and knew enough to keep quiet. Noles was a second-year pro at the time and was in the midst of a miserable season, which would end with a 4–16 record and a 5.91 ERA for a last-place team.

"Dickie Noles and I later got to be great friends," said Joe. "But that day was some welcome to pro ball. I learned two things that day. One was to keep my mouth shut and listen, and the other was not to mess with Dickie Noles."

Joe's first professional game was against the Ashville Rangers. He was the leadoff man for Spartanburg and played centerfield.

"The Phillies still thought I was fast," said Joe. "My first time up, I faced Danny Darwin, who now pitches for Texas. He struck me out. I grounded out in my next at bat. I remember thinking that I would give anything to get a hit in that first game. I prayed for a bloop, a broken bat single, a bunt, anything."

In his third at bat, Joe faced a different pitcher. Darwin had given way to Paul Mirabella, a left-hander now with Toronto. Joe grounded a base hit between short and third base.

During those early days, Joe was platooned in centerfield with left-hand-hitting Kenny Berger.

"Berger and I had this big rivalry," said Joe. "He was this intense Jewish guy from Florida, and he wanted to be a regular. Well, I wanted to play all the time, too. I thought I had to hit .300 or I couldn't face my friends back home. I had told them that I was going to hit .300 that first year."

After a month at Spartanburg, Joe's average was hovering at the .240 mark. Even though he did not make an error that season, Spartanburg Manager Lee Elia would tell him that he had a coronary watching him trying to catch fly balls. Things were not going well.

Off the field, it was another story.

Charboneau shared a two-bedroom apartment with four other Spartanburg players. From his $500-a-month salary, Joe was clearing a little more than $300 after taxes. He and his four roommates shared the $300 rent on the apartment.

Joe was taking part in all that goes with being away from home for the first time. He would stay up until 4 A.M. and then sleep until 3 P.M., setting the alarm so he would rise in time for his daily soap opera, "General Hospital."

"When I first moved in with those guys, they put me on the couch," said Joe. "The place was an incredible mess. The carpet was never vacuumed. You couldn't even see it because of all the newspapers, pieces of old pizzas, chicken bones, candy wrappers and other junk scattered about.

"In the bathroom, the wet floor was matted down with pictures from *Playboy*," continued Joe. "The place was filthy, and it smelled."

The players adopted a stray dog.

"We called him Rat because he was so ugly," said Joe. "For a week, he slept with me on the couch. Then he left. We were too dirty even for Rat, and that is hard to believe because Rat had mange. The other guys would never let me forget that I had slept with a mangy dog."

It was not uncommon for most players to stay up all night, like Joe, though there was little to do but watch TV and drink beer. They had no extra money, and that put a severe cramp in their recreational options. Keith Gale was one of Joe's roommates. He was usually the last of the crew to go to sleep. He spent his nights writing letters.

"I remember getting so mad at Gale because he wouldn't shut off the light and go to bed that I threw a tennis shoe at him," said Charboneau. "I missed but the shoe put a hole in the wall."

Stacking four or five players in an apartment is a usual practice in the low Minors. Beds are issued on a seniority system, according to who has been in the apartment the longest. When one of Joe's roommates was released, Joe finally moved off the couch and into a bed. The new player who was brought in was given Joe's old sleeping quarters.

Loneliness is a major foe at this level of baseball. A girlfriend in town is a status symbol, because not many women are willing to socialize with scared young Minor Leaguers. Only a few players had cars, extra money or any of the social graces.

"The guys in our apartment were lucky," said Joe. "One of my roommates was a guy named Jim Nickerson. He was a big, fat pitcher. I'd say he was 6-foot-2, 230 pounds. He was from Pittsburg, Texas. His father owned a huge ranch and a private jet. Jim was always calling home and asking about their cows. He loved those cows."

Nickerson was considered Minor League royalty because he owned a car. Often, he would pile his roommates into the automobile, and they would go to a movie. Then they would all go out for steaks.

"Nickerson loved steaks," said Joe. "If a guy didn't have enough money for a movie or steaks, Nickerson would take care of it. He was a great guy."

The father of Jim Nickerson was also a hit. He would fly up in his jet to watch his son pitch. He liked to take some of the Spartanburg players up for rides in the jet after games. The Spartanburg team was convinced that the Nickerson family owned all of Pittsburg (population—3,800).

This band of Minor Leaguers was not without its quirks and spats.

"One day we made mashed potatoes," said Joe. "It was probably one of the two home-cooked meals we made all summer. Anyhow, after the dinner was over, we got into this argument about who should clear the table. Nobody wanted to do it. So we left the potatoes sitting there."

According to Charboneau, the potatoes remained on the table for six weeks, until Cindy came to visit Joe. "When Cindy threw them out, they had mold and other green stuff hanging from them, as long as the hair on your head," recalled Joe.

They also bickered about taking out the garbage. Finally, this issue was settled in the same manner as the potatoes.

"We just let the stuff stack up in the corner of the kitchen," said Joe. "Then a couple of guys bought some white mice for pets. The mice ate their way out of their boxes, so we put them in the garbage and hoped that they would eat it."

The pile of debris was beyond the rodents, however.

"Mostly, the mice just roamed the apartment," said Joe. "They would crawl on you while you were sleeping. The last straw came when they ate a hole in Nickerson's shaving kit. That was it. Nickerson said they had to go.

"Our apartment was on the second floor. Someone got the idea to throw them out the window. So we dropped these mice down a story and figured that was the end of them. A few minutes later, the neighbor below us knocked on our door. He said he thought these mice were ours and handed them to us. We had them another week before we gave them away."

Nickerson loved air conditioning, and Joe claims that he always kept the rooms at 40 or 50 degrees.

"Joe would always say he was cold," said Frank Lucy, who roomed with Charboneau on the road. "When we got to a hotel, the first thing he would do is take all the covers and sheets off the bed. Then he would wrap himself up in them and sleep in this cocoon on the stripped bed. He would stay like that for hours, and I always had to wake him up or he would be late for the games."

Joe likes to swap tall stories and do bizarre things. One of his classic stunts began in a bar in Spartanburg. Joe was sitting around with Jim Nickerson and a few other players. Charboneau and Nickerson would never win any awards for modesty, and on this night they were swapping weird tales.

Finally, Joe blurted out, "I can drink beer through my nose."

There was silence. After all, this was a serious boast.

"Nah, I don't believe it," said Nickerson.

Joe had already opened a bottle of beer with his forearm; and on one other night he had opened a bottle with his eye socket, "but that hurt like hell and left a scar under my right eyebrow."

Actually, Joe had never consumed beer through his nose before that night in Spartanburg. But as he poured it down his nose, and later sipped some through a nostril with a straw, yet another Super Joe legend was born.

"I'd never done that before," said Joe. "But I always thought I could. I had had my nose messed up so many times in the past that there was no cartilage left in there."

"Everybody called Joe 'The Kid,'" said Frank Lucy. "He fashioned himself as a tough boxer, and he loved to tell all those stories, cutting out his tattoo, fighting in boxcars and drinking beer through his nose. The word got around the team quick. You just had to go with 'The Kid' and hear those incredible stories."

In mid-July, Cindy Engle flew to Spartanburg to visit Joe.

"I could not believe their apartment," said Cindy. "It is impossible that anybody could live in anything as dirty as that. They let mashed potatoes sit on the kitchen table for six weeks. It was repulsive."

When most of Joe's roommates had visitors, they did not bring them to the apartment, for obvious reasons. During her stay, Cindy tried to straighten the place up, but found the task harder than getting

Joe to awaken before noon. She spent four days cleaning two of the four rooms, the living room and the kitchen.

Cindy's arrival did help Joe's performance on the field. His batting average rose from .240 to .270 while she attended the games, and he had one 10-for-12 streak.

"Those guys seemed like a bunch of little boys with no cares or responsibilities," said Cindy. "They stayed up all night, slept all day and never picked up after themselves."

"When Cindy came, I took her on a picnic with some of the other players," said Joe. "We took a boat ride on this lake, and as she got out of the boat in shallow water, this water moccasin brushed by her leg. I grabbed an oar and beat it to death. After I was through, Nickerson took the oar and beat it some more."

"Little boys," said Cindy, recalling the incident.

At the ballpark, Joe's performance continued to improve after Cindy returned to Santa Clara. He was still being platooned with Kenny Berger, but he was making more of his opportunities.

"When Joe first got to Spartanburg, I think he was happy just to get signed," said Frank Lucy. "The Phillies never liked him much, and they couldn't figure him out because he is different from most ballplayers. They didn't like the way he wore his cap, just sitting on top of his head instead of pulled down over his eyes. They thought he messed around too much and wasn't serious about playing. The opposite was true. After a bad day, he would go back to our hotel room and stay up all night swinging his bat, trying to figure out what went wrong."

Another way Joe dealt with a poor outing was to walk off his anger and frustration. It was a five-mile hike from the Spartanburg ballpark to Charboneau's apartment, and it was not uncommon for Joe to cover that trek on foot, when things didn't go well. Coping with the pressures of being a professional, and watching those who failed be released and sent home, took a toll on Joe. He worried, and worried often. His confidence was like a rubber band on the verge of snapping.

"The whole Minor League scene got to me," said Joe. "I wasn't playing all the time, and I was away from home. That first year is a rough time for anyone, especially on the road."

Spartanburg traveled by bus. The driver was a man named Charlie Royals.

"I loved Charlie," said Joe. "He also was our team trainer, and he took good care of me. But he was something else. First of all, he always had a cigar in his mouth. Second, he was always cussing. He couldn't say a sentence without including 'damns' and stuff. And he always acted grouchy. I remember that he would always grind the gears of the bus."

In addition to Spartanburg, the other members of the Western Carolina League were Ashville (N.C.), Greenwood (S.C.) and Charleston (S.C.).

"We always stayed in rotten motels," said Joe. "Most of them were clean, but that was the best you could hope for. We got $6.50 a day for meal money on the road, and no one can eat three meals on $6.50. Most of us ate only once or twice a day, and most of our food came from places like McDonald's."

On one of those trips, Joe found himself in the middle of a Charleston ghetto. He was not hitting, and could not venture outside his room for fear of having someone try to dislodge his head from his shoulders. It was a Saturday night in August. Joe reached for the telephone and called Cindy.

"Hello," said Cindy.

"I'm so lonely," said Joe. "Let's get married. You can come and stay with me."

There was a moment of silence.

"Okay," said Cindy.

And that was it; Joe had proposed after going 0-for-4.

"If it weren't for baseball, I don't think we would have gotten married," said Cindy. "We had never discussed it before, and I certainly wasn't counting on him asking me. I was planning to go to college and keep up with my swimming. But when he asked, I could not turn him down."

Following his decision to marry Cindy, Joe was revived. He finished the year on a tear, missing by only two points his goal of .300. In 121 at bats, he had four homers and 18 RBIs. He also proved conclusively that his speed was nothing more than a pleasant memory by stealing but one base.

In 1976, the Western Carolina League featured several players, in addition to Joe, who would one day play in the Majors. Among them were Danny Darwin (now with Texas), Paul Mirabella (Toronto), Nelson Norman (Texas), Dickie Noles (Philadelphia), Dale Berra (Pittsburgh) and Jose Moreno (Mets). The leading hitter in the league was Pat Putnam, the current Rangers first baseman. He was selected the top player in all of Minor League baseball, as he batted .361 with 24 homers and 142 RBIs in 138 games.

Joe's friendly adversary, Kenny Berger, batted .249 with five homers, while Joe's roommate Jim Nickerson, was 2–4 with a 4.46 ERA.

Following that first season, the Phillies considered Joe a strong enough prospect to invite him to their winter Instructional League club in Clearwater, Florida. The Instructional League is designed for teams to bring their best young Minor Leaguers together for six weeks of intense teaching and exhibition games.

"Nothing big happened to me in the Instructional League, except that I was bitten by a turtle and almost attacked by an alligator," said Joe.

The turtle incident took place when Joe and some of his teammates went skinny-dipping in a Florida river. A snapping turtle tried to take a hunk out of Joe's toe. Joe still has a small scar from the occurrence, and he will not go into a lake or the ocean without wearing tennis shoes. "I do learn from experience," he maintains.

As for the incident with the gator, Joe says, "I was in a car with a couple of players, and we were in the middle of nowhere. I had to go to the bathroom, so I told them to stop the car and I would take a leak by this swamp. I was standing there, just starting to go, when what I thought was a log, moved. It was an alligator, and its tail hit my leg. I zipped up my pants, getting them all wet because I hadn't finished, and ran back to the car."

Charboneau was anxious for the winter league season to come to a close because he wanted to return home and marry Cindy.

The wedding was held January 15, 1977, at St. Justin's Catholic Church in Santa Clara. It was the same church Joe had attended as a youngster, and Cindy went along with a Catholic wedding even though she was not a member of the Church.

"We had about 350 people at our reception," said Joe. "They were all friends and relatives. My brothers and sisters made it, but my father couldn't. The reception was held at the La Hacienda Inn. All night we had nothing to eat or drink because we spent all our time greeting people. The only thing we ate was the first piece of cake."

At the same time as the Charboneau reception, the Inn was also the site of a party attended by baseball great Joe DiMaggio.

"I always tell people that Joe DiMaggio came to my wedding," said Joe. "Well, I did see him across the hall."

Following the wedding, Joe and Cindy left for a honeymoon in the Northwest, where they spent two weeks visiting Joe's brothers and Cindy's father at Crater Lake. When they returned to Santa Clara, they moved in with Mrs. Charboneau. Cindy got a job at McDonalds, while Joe worked out, living off the remainder of his bonus money.

7 ★★★★★★

PENINSULA

The Phillies still seemed very pleased with Charboneau. In addition to sending him to their Winter Instructional League club, they also gave him a 1977 contract calling for $750 a month.´ That was a $250-a-month increase, which is considered a hefty raise by Minor League standards, especially since Joe was again to play in Class A.

"That spring they finally realized that I couldn't run anymore," said Joe. "They switched me from center to leftfield and also used me as a designated hitter."

After spring training, Philadelphia assigned Joe to its Peninsula farm club. Peninsula is a member of the Carolina League. While still a Class A league, the Carolina League's quality of play is far superior to that of the Western Carolina League, where Joe performed in 1976. In the Carolina League, most of the players have two to three years of professional experience, while one year was the norm in the Western Carolina League.

"It looked like things were going to work out," said Joe. "I was going to be the starting leftfielder. I was excited."

Cindy spent the spring with Joe in Clearwater, Florida, and then she drove their VW Superbeetle to Newport News, Virginia, where Peninsula is located. They found an apartment, and then Joe decided that there was a missing ingredient.

"We need a dog," Joe said to Cindy. "It will keep you company when I go on the road."

The Charboneaus traveled to the local animal shelter. One of the first cages they passed contained a month-old German shepherd.

"Every time we walked away from him, he cried," said Joe. "Cindy really liked him. He was cute, but he was so young. They said he had been abused and beaten by his previous owner."

Joe paid $20 for the dog and his shots. During the ride back to their apartment, they found a name for the puppy.

"He crapped all over the car," said Joe. "I mean, he never seemed to stop going from the moment he got into the car. We called him Diarrhea, Rhea for short. We still have the dog. Rhea lives with Cindy's mother in San Jose."

Perhaps Joe was being a bit presumptuous in his purchase of a puppy and plans for a great Minor League season. He talked of hitting at least .300 and maybe moving up to Class AA by July. Charboneau began the year by going 3-for-17 and soon found himself out of the lineup.

"Suddenly, it seemed like they didn't like me anymore," said Joe. "Granted, I didn't start well, but after 17 at-bats they took me out of the lineup and acted as if I didn't exist."

"Joe may not have realized it, but the Phillies weren't thrilled with him," said Frank Lucy, a teammate of Charboneau's in Spartanburg and Peninsula. "The Phillies have a certain way of doing things. They didn't like people with different personalities or attitudes. They always stressed that you had to act and think a certain way if you wanted to be a Phillie. This was especially true for guys like Joe, who didn't get a big bonus. Joe's major problem with Philadelphia was that he was a different kind of guy. When he had a slump, he found out what they actually thought of him."

"After they took me out of the lineup, they decided that they had to do something about my throwing," said Joe. "I have always had a bad arm. I hurt my shoulder playing football in high school, and I haven't thrown that great since. Well, the Phillies thought that the best way to strengthen my arm was to make me throw and throw from the outfield. I would tell them that my arm was killing me, and they would make me throw some more."

"The Phillies almost used the throwing practice as a punishment for Joe," said Frank Lucy. "They would make him throw while everyone else was taking batting practice. That would really get to Joe, because he loved to hit more than anything else. Joe just had a lousy arm, and all the throwing in the world wasn't going to change it."

"I began to wonder if they still considered me a prospect," said Charboneau. "You don't take a player you think is a prospect and make him throw until it seems that his arm is going to fall off. I worked hard for the Phillies. I was willing to stay after practice and work some more on my throwing, but I liked to get my batting practice in, and they wouldn't let me."

When a player is sitting on the bench and feels he is being singled out for some sort of sadistic punishment under the guise of helping him improve, paranoia sets in. He begins to believe that the Major League organization does not want him to succeed, that they are seeking any excuse to cut him. He thinks that nothing he does is good enough and that he is doomed. It is baseball's version of the convict on Death Row, awaiting the inevitable and deplorable end. To a ballplayer, being released is a form of death, because his life is baseball.

"During the time Joe wasn't playing, he walked around in this daze," said Cindy. "He wouldn't say that much. Mostly he would mope around. He thought that the Phillies were trying to break him."

On several occasions, Joe went to see his manager, Jim Snyder. He asked why he was on the bench, and Snyder replied that Joe did not hit when he was given the opportunity. Now it was someone else's turn.

"What kind of chance is 17 at-bats?" Joe would ask the manager time and time again. Snyder would shrug and say little, and Joe still would not play.

"The thing Joe didn't understand was that decisions about who played and who didn't were made by the Phillies front office," said Lucy. "Snyder would tell Joe that his hands were tied, but Joe didn't understand. Not playing was killing him. He was so hurt, so confused. He had a rough time dealing with the situation."

In the Minor Leagues, it is not uncommon for the front office to tell the manager to start certain people and give him the batting order. A Minor League manager who says to the front office that he will make the decisions about who plays will not remain a Minor League manager for very long.

Most front offices view the situation from the standpoint that they are the boss. They pay the salaries of the players and manager. They have certain players they want to get experience, because they feel that these athletes are the most likely to one day be Major Leaguers, even though they may not be the best at their respective positions on their Minor League club. "Development" and "the future" are the words spoken most often in Major League farm departments. Their function is to turn out the most Major League players possible. Winning on the Minor League level is secondary to nurturing players.

There is a prejudice built into this system. In most cases, if a player is drafted high and has received a large bonus, he is considered a Major League prospect until he proves himself totally inept in what often seems like countless trials. When a big league club invests fifty to a hundred thousand dollars in an athlete, they want to make sure that he has every opportunity to prove the scouts correct in their high assessment of his ability. A player with a small bonus usually receives far fewer chances to display his talents.

"The Phillies were very patient with the bonus babies, even when their attitudes or personalities weren't the best," said Frank Lucy. "But a guy who was considered a marginal player when he was signed had better keep his mouth shut and his nose clean."

Patience is not a virtue with Joe Charboneau. He wanted to play, and he wanted to play now, and he didn't care if Babe Ruth was playing in front of him. While he won't admit it, when he was not in the lineup, he pouted, and this enraged the Phillies. As for his reaction to his exile on the bench, Joe alternated between fits of screaming and terrifying silences.

"Toward the end, Joe got very rebellious," said Frank Lucy. "When he was told to do something, he would purposely do the opposite just to piss people off. He would yell a lot, asking to be traded."

The one stunt which signaled his divorce from the Philadelphia organization had to be repeated several times. It broke a cardinal rule of athletes at any level. The canon is that an athlete is never to quit. Sports is like a war, where surrender is not an option. Supposedly, there is an excuse for everything in professional sports, short of giving up.

Although he was under severe pressure and the Phillies were as sympathetic as concentration camp guards, Joe quit, and that made him a non-person in the world of baseball.

"In games where he didn't play, Joe left the field a couple of times before they were over," said Frank Lucy. "He would go in the seventh or eighth inning. He just was so disgusted that he felt he had to do something, and his answer was to leave."

"I remember that some members of the Phillies told me that Joe didn't quit once, he did it several times," said Cleveland Indians Scout Dan Carnevale. "They said he was real trouble."

"I was just tired of everything," said Joe. "In those games where I left the field, I knew that I wasn't going to pinch-hit under any circumstances. I felt useless. So I walked out, went into the clubhouse, changed into my street clothes and sat there."

At this point, the Phillies and Charboneau had reached the end. They considered him an ungrateful basket case, not worthy of wearing a Phillies uniform. He thought they were stupid and unfeeling, blind to his talent and bent on destroying his career.

"I asked them to send me back down to Spartanburg where I could play every day, and they refused," said Charboneau. "So I asked them to trade me, or even release me, so I could find an organization that wanted me. They refused again. They said that they wanted me to stay right where I was. I was on the bench with no hope of playing."

"Joe was the black sheep, in the doghouse, or whatever you wanted to call it," said Frank Lucy.

Lucy and the rest of Charboneau's Peninsula teammates were not the only ones who knew that Joe's relationship with the Phillies was approaching the explosive stage. Joe was also well aware that something had to be done. He often discussed the problem with Cindy, and their conversations went along these lines:

"What do you think I should do?" asked Joe.

"You're the only one who knows," said Cindy.

"It looks to me like I'm through. I'm never going to get to the Majors this way," said Joe.

"You still love baseball, don't you?" asked Cindy.

"Yes," said Joe.

"So you must be sure what you do is right for you," said Cindy.

"Right now, I feel that the only thing I can do is quit," said Joe.

For over a week this conversation took various forms. The first time Joe brought the subject up, he was prepared to walk out the next day. Cindy convinced him to wait another week. Then one day he went to the park and found his name in the lineup.

"I wanted to play more than anything," said Joe. "But my arm was killing me because of all the throwing. I thought that this was it. I had no arm. That day, I had to tell Jim Snyder that my arm hurt too much to play, and I could tell then that I would never play again. The situation seemed hopeless. Here I was, finally supposed to play, and I couldn't because of what they did to my arm. They had no intention of playing me long enough to see what I could do."

Charboneau returned to the park the following day and told the Phillies that he was going to quit if they would not trade or release him. They said they had no plans to let him go, but that he should go home and spend another day thinking about his retirement.

"I went back to the park the following day, and I had not changed my mind," said Joe. "Then I found out that I had been fined $250 and was suspended because I had a bad attitude. I just walked away from it, and I was happy to leave."

The 1977 baseball season was barely a month old, but it was over for Joe. The Phillies kept him on their suspended list, meaning he could not sign with another team. In essence, his choice was to play at Peninsula or not at all.

"I felt relieved after I decided to quit," said Joe. "That week when I was thinking about what to do was one of the worst times of my life. The really bad part about all this was that my mother was visiting relatives in Florida at the time, and then she was planning to come up to Peninsula to see me play. Since there was no telephone where she was staying, I sent her a telegram and told her not to come. She called me and asked me what happened. I told her that I was coming home."

At this juncture, Joe was convinced that he would not play another game of professional baseball. He and Cindy packed their 1973

Volkswagen with everything they owned, including their new puppy, and began their journey across the country.

"The car was so jammed that I could not see out the back window," said Joe. "I drove home in twenty-six straight hours. The ride was fun. We talked about everything but baseball. We both were happy and excited about starting a new life."

Charboneau's decision to retire was greeted with a yawn by most of his teammates. In the low Minors, players come and go all the time. It was not unusual for a Class A club to be a revolving door, running through 40 players during the course of the year because of players being promoted, sent down or released. Only a few quit.

"The other players liked Joe a lot," said Frank Lucy. "But a lot of us were not surprised when he came to the park one day and said that he was packing his bags and going home because he couldn't take it anymore. The guys felt bad for Joe because he had no airs. He was a genuine guy. The Phillies were the only people who didn't understand him. It began with his cap. He wore it tilted up on top of his head, and they thought it looked cocky. They didn't have much patience with him. It was like they set out to break him. In the end, they did."

Listening to Frank Lucy's remarks about the Phillies, one must consider that he too is not thrilled with the organization. A native of Bedford, Ohio, who attended Arizona State, Lucy was traded by Philadelphia to Detroit's Class AA Montgomery farm club in 1979 and then released before the 1980 season. Like Charboneau, Lucy believes that the Phillies did not treat him fairly.

Charboneau's final totals for 1977 show that he batted 29 times, hit one homer and had a .172 average.

8 ★★★★★★

QUITTING

The trip home was bliss for Joe and Cindy Charboneau, but their arrival brought on fear, panic and doubt. The lingering question was, "Now what?"

Now what should they do?

Now what should they feel?

Now what will happen?

For the first time in his life, Joe had to go out and find a job. No, he needed a career. He had had other jobs, the most notable being his time with TOYS-R-US. But that was just a stopgap, something to fill the time and give him a few bucks before he began playing baseball for a living. Yes, there was a significant difference. You play baseball, but everything else is work. A ballplayer goes to the park, not to the plant or office. Those who play baseball and don't love it are considered freaks, while those who toil in other fields and admit to liking their jobs are called workaholics.

"It broke my heart when Joe quit baseball, and I'm sure he felt the same way," said Mrs. Charboneau. "But Joe is not a stupid boy. He may have done some crazy things, but in the end, he always did what was right."

"I knew that I had to get out of baseball," said Joe. "But that was about all I knew. I had no idea what to do. Cindy and I moved in with my mother and my younger brother, John. Cindy got a job right away as an assembler at an electrical plant. I couldn't find anything. In that first month, we collected food stamps. It was the first time we ever went on welfare. We were on it for a month until I got a job."

Joe was finally employed in the stock room of an electrical plant.

"I got the job because of my sister and brother-in-law," said Joe. "They made it seem like I got the job on my own, which was very nice of them, but they set it up for me. I started at $3.75 an hour."

Then began the search. Joe was empty and lost. He had an aching void. Baseball had occupied such a large part of his thoughts and time. Now, he was like an artist without his paint, a fisherman without his net or a farmer without his soil. Joe was a player without his game.

"After I quit, I hated baseball," said Joe. "I would not watch a game on television or read the sports page. Cindy and I tried karate, but I quit after three weeks when she turned out to be a lot better at it than me."

"I was happy to be back home because it gave me a chance to get back to my swimming," said Cindy. "I would come home from work, throw dinner on the table for Joe and then go out and swim. We hardly talked. Joe spent a lot of time talking with his mother."

"He wouldn't admit it, but I knew that Joe missed baseball," said Mrs. Charboneau. "He was so restless. He was looking for something."

"I had all this energy," said Joe. "I needed something more than my job. My brother Rick is a weight-lifter, and he got me very interested in that. I would spend a couple hours each night after work lifting. On Saturdays, I would go four hours at a time. The man who sold me the weights owned this sporting goods store, and he thought I had the makings of a professional body-builder. I became a physical-fitness freak. I would do 500 sit-ups a day, run five miles, and I was bench-pressing between 360 and 390 pounds. I got up to 401 pounds once."

The bending and the sweating and the grunting and the pursuit of doing more sit-ups or lifting more weights acted like methadone to a drug addict for Joe. He was gradually weaning himself away from baseball.

Charboneau handled the withdrawal in sullen silence. He said little, and Cindy occupied herself with working and swimming to the point that she was not around to listen had he decided to speak.

"I feel very bad about not having been more in tune with Joe's emotions," said Cindy. "I really didn't notice that he was having a bad time."

Joe's rage manifested itself just once.

"Something trivial happened. I don't even remember what it was," said Joe. "I got super upset. I had this roll of tape in my hand, and I flung it with all my might at the glass sliding door. It broke the glass. I ended up having to work overtime to get money to fix it."

Joe was just beginning to think that he did not need baseball when brother Rick came up with what appeared to be a perfectly innocent invitation.

"We need somebody to play on our softball team," said Rick Charboneau.

"I don't know," said Joe.

"Hell, you won't even have to play under your own name," said Rick. "You can play for this guy, Randy Butts. Try it. If you don't like it, you only have to play this once."

Two months after walking away from his professional baseball career, Charboneau stepped on to a dusty, rutted diamond. The players wore T-shirts, jeans and tennis shoes for uniforms. It was a classic beer league, with the men being far more concerned about the postgame six-packs than the final score.

"In that first game, Joe hit three grand slam homers," said Rick Charboneau. "I know it is hard to believe, but it's true. He was awesome. The funny thing was that Randy Butts had been batting about .100 when Joe took his place."

"I really got into those games," said Joe. "I couldn't wait for Thursday to come so I could play. The league was nothing. Just some fat guys having a good time. If you could hit and run a little bit, you had no problem."

So it was. Joe Charboneau spent his days as a shipping-and-receiving clerk and his nights were filled with weights. In between there was a little softball and a lot of depression. Then, one winter day, he received a telephone call from his mother. Joe was at work and happy for something to break the routine.

"Joe, you got a letter from the Phillies," said Mrs. Charboneau.

"Ah, it's probably my release," said Joe.

"I don't think so," said his mother. "It seems pretty thick."

"Go ahead and open it," said Joe.

"It's a contract," said Mrs. Charboneau.

After hanging up, Mrs. Charboneau said a prayer of thanks and asked the Lord to help Joe decide to sign the document. Her eyes were filled with tears of joy.

Meanwhile, Charboneau could not wait until he got off from work. When he did, he rushed home and looked at the contract. Then he went to his bedroom and picked up his professional bat for the first time since his retirement. He held it in his hands for several minutes. Then he and his brothers went out and played baseball.

"But I still wasn't sure if I should sign," said Joe. "I had a decent future at the electrical plant. Every day I would come and ask my mother and Cindy if I should sign, and they would say it was up to me."

"Mrs. Charboneau and I both wanted Joe to try baseball again, and we knew he wanted to sign," said Cindy. "But we were going to let it be his decision."

A few weeks after Joe received the contract, Eddie Bockman called Joe, and the two planned a luncheon date.

"I couldn't figure out what had happened to Joe," said Bockman. "The kids I sign don't quit. I don't sign that kind of kid. Joe was right out of the mold of players I sign, like Larry Bowa. They are hungry and aggressive. Joe is the same way. We talked about what happened several times, and he said that he still thought he could play in the Majors, but he would never find out on the bench."

Bockman spoke with Philadelphia Minor League Director Dallas Green about Charboneau. Bockman recommended that Joe be given another chance, and Green concurred by mailing out the $750-a-month Class A contract. Green also suggested that Bockman meet with Joe and tell him what to expect in spring training.

"Over lunch, Eddie Bockman told me that if I signed there was no guarantee that I would make it through spring training," said Joe. "He said I was going to be the black sheep, and that it would be tougher than ever for me. He told me that I was going to have to control my temper and keep my mouth shut. He said this was my last chance."

Joe still had not decided if he should return.

Then he began to think. He remembered getting his first baseball glove and sleeping with it. He remembered selling frogs so he could buy his first pair of spikes. He remembered sleeping with his baseball bat. He remembered how he did not want to take off his uniform after his last high school game. These things mold a man, just like those boxcar brawls taught him to fight and never, ever, to quit. Charboneau is a product of all this. They are the ingredients of his heart and mind.

"He continued to ask me every day if he should sign," said Cindy. "I got tired of being noncommittal. Finally, I said that if he ever wanted to know for sure if he could have made the big leagues, he should sign."

That was enough for Joe. He returned the contract with his signature to the Phillies the next day.

"When Joe signed, it was probably the happiest day of my life," said Mrs. Charboneau. "He missed baseball more than he ever realized. He is not a 9–5 type guy. He is a ballplayer. That's all he ever wanted to be."

9 ★★★★★★★

VISALIA

Joe Charboneau had been warned that spring training would not be a snap, but he did not think that this also applied to his airplane ride. As Joe departed from San Jose for the Phillies' Florida quarters in Clearwater, the plane immediately developed trouble.

"There was something wrong with one of the engines or something," said Joe. "They said not to worry. We just had to make an emergency landing in San Francisco."

An emergency landing? "No problem," Joe Charboneau was told. That is like saying, "Now don't be concerned, but with your next step you may set off a land mine."

"Actually, everything did go pretty smoothly," said Joe. "We went down in San Francisco, and they said the plane would not be ready to leave for another eight hours. We took off at midnight and landed in Clearwater at 7 A.M."

When Joe went to the Clearwater airport luggage rack, he found another surprise.

"They lost everything, my spikes, glove, my clothes and my bats. For three days I wore the same clothes, and I smelled like it. I had to borrow gloves, spikes and bats from other players. It was not a great way to start."

What further upset Joe was the news that he had been assigned to play under Jim Snyder. That was the same Jim Snyder who had managed Peninsula in 1977, and the same Jim Snyder with, Joe thought, as much compassion and understanding as Attila the Hun.

"It was something else," said Joe. "The only players who would talk to me were the guys I knew before. Everybody else avoided me like I had a disease or something. Obviously, they had been told that I was a troublemaker and to stay away from me. It was not a good feeling."

For two weeks of exhibition games, Joe was a nonentity. He batted but four times and had three hits. "I figured that I would be called into the office any day and told that I was being released," said Joe. "I was expecting it. It seemed as though they had no plans for me. I couldn't even figure out why they had invited me back."

One day, Joe was waved into the office. Philadelphia Minor League Administrator Howie Bedell told him to sit down.

"I thought I was through," said Joe.

Bedell told Charboneau that he was being outrighted to the Minnesota Twins Class A Visalia club. He was to report to the Twins spring training camp in Melbourne, Florida. For a moment, Joe was confused. He thought he had been traded, but that was not the case.

While Joe would play for a Minnesota farm team and wear a Twins' uniform, he would remain property of the Phillies, and Philadelphia would also pay his salary. Essentially, Joe was being loaned to the Twins' Visalia club, and the Phillies could send him to one of their farm teams any time. For a ballplayer, being outrighted is the final step before being cut. It means that your organization does not consider you worthy enough to play for one of their clubs, but they are not quite ready to send you home. It is a perilous situation, like living with a pacemaker which could be shut off at any moment.

"I took the news pretty well," said Joe. "I was told that Visalia needed another outfielder and that I would get a chance to play. All I ever wanted was to play so I could show them what I could do. Visalia is only three hours from Santa Clara, so it was nice to be close to home."

Once Charboneau joined Visalia, he felt like suing the Phillies for false advertising. They did not need another outfielder, and he seemed like nothing more than excess baggage.

"I did not play in the first ten games," said Joe. "I was ready to quit again. I was not going to sit on the bench. Cindy and I talked about moving to Holland. She had a chance to be a swimming coach there, and I could become a body-builder."

The man keeping Joe in cold storage was a fellow named Dan Henry. The Visalia starting leftfielder, Henry, was called "Potatohead" by his teammates, for obvious reasons. Potatohead was forced to the bench with a pulled leg muscle, and Joe was inserted into the lineup for the first time in Game No. 11 of the 1978 season.

"We played a doubleheader," said Joe. "The first game went extra innings, and I was 1-for-6, my only hit being a drag bunt. Then I got hot. Over the next three games, I was 10-for-13 with two homers, six doubles and a triple."

From that point on, Joe was the leftfielder and batted fifth. Visalia was an awesome club, winning its first 14 games and finishing the year with a 97–42 record. Early in the season, Joe told a Visalia reporter that he would bat .350, with 100 RBIs and 100 runs scored along with 20 homers. He would indeed bat .350, drive in 116 runs and score 119. He fell a bit short in the home run estimate, ending up with 18.

"I had the best time at Visalia that I ever had playing baseball," said Joe. "The players on the team were really close. We always had parties, and we were a real clan. These guys believed that the team which drank and partied together stayed together."

Cindy and Joe rented a two-bedroom apartment in Visalia for $230 a month. They shared it with Visalia teammate John Daynor.

"It was a neat place," said Cindy. "We still hadn't bought any furniture, but we rented a bed, a couch and a bean bag chair. We had no table, so we ate on the floor. We hung three posters on the walls. One was a Barreta poster, another said YOU ARE A NERD and the third said MUPPET POWER. We made a pyramid of empty beer cans and stacked them against the wall. When Joe wasn't hitting, he would come home and knock down the pyramid, and then we would spend most of the next day putting it back up."

Things were going so well for Joe that he decided to buy himself a birthday surprise.

"I can't walk by a pet shop without stopping in," said Joe. "I always wanted something out of the ordinary. Our dog, Rhea, was with Cindy's mom. In this pet shop, I saw a baby alligator. It was my birthday so I said, 'What the hell, I'm going to get myself a present.'"

The gator was eight inches on June 17, 1978, when it joined the Charboneau household. Joe paid $20 for it, but he was shocked to discover that the tank required to hold it cost $80.

"I really didn't care how much it was. I wanted it," said Joe. "I heard that you could teach alligators tricks, and hypnotize them by rubbing their stomachs. We named our gator Chopper."

"Joe really liked Chopper," said Cindy. "He worried about him being warm enough. He would put a pillow around the air conditioner near Chopper's tank so he wouldn't catch a cold."

"I liked to feed him," said Joe. "He ate crickets and goldfish. We would buy the fish and catch the crickets. You are only supposed to feed an alligator twice a week, but I would do it about five times because he seemed hungry all the time."

Chopper was the star of the many parties hosted by the Charboneaus.

"We always had cookouts and stuff like that," said Joe. "We would fill the bathtub with ice and beer, and invite the team over. The party would always start by feeding Chopper. The guys really enjoyed watching him eat. He'd swallow a goldfish or a cricket, and everybody would cheer."

"Once, we had a costume party," said Cindy. "Joe dressed up as a fairy and had on lace and a long blond wig which went down to his rear. Another player showed up in a strait jacket and a third wore a cheerleading skirt."

The parties were riotous fun for Joe and his friends, but they made Chopper a confused and ornery alligator.

"A lot of people would tease him," said Joe. "I tried to play with him and show him tricks, and he would bite me. He hated my guts for some reason. One time, he bit me on my left thumb down to the bone.

I still have the scar. I wanted to train him to wrestle. Gators grow about a foot each of their first six years. In six years, he would have been my size, and we could have had a great time."

"Chopper got to be a pain," said Cindy. "Joe was always going out and catching crickets to feed him. But the end came when Joe was on the road. I was taking care of Chopper and a kitten that one of Joe's teammates left at our place. Somehow, the top got knocked off Chopper's tank, and the kitten had its paw inside. Chopper was getting ready to bite it off when I pulled the kitten out. I told Joe when he got home that Chopper had to go."

Joe gave Chopper to teammate Jerry Ennis. Chopper was about three pounds and 20 inches long when he left the Charboneau household.

The alligator met a bitter end. One day, Ennis was cleaning Chopper's tank, and he left the gator in the bathtub. Apparently, something startled Chopper, because he jumped up and conked his head on the faucet. He was killed instantly.

At times, Joe and his teammates moved their parties to the local pubs. One such outing made Charboneau a legend in the California League.

The Tapper Bar of Visalia was a typical beer-and-a-shot joint. Picnic tables and benches were the furniture. The frills were a pool table and a jukebox with nothing but country music. This waterhole served beer in bottles, cans and foam-filled mugs. The place catered to a clientele which was best described as ridiculously redneck.

Cindy, Joe and five other Visalia players entered the Tapper. Joe left Cindy at the bar, while he and his friends headed to a corner.

"We got into this contest," said Joe. "You drink a beer and then try to rip the T-shirt off another guy's back. It's a little rough, but good clean fun."

One Visalia player downed a brew and then went for Joe's shirt. Off it came. For good measure, he bit Joe on the shoulder. Joe laughed. A Willie Nelson song was coming from the jukebox and sounded so sweet and so good. The beer was wet and cold and right.

Meanwhile, Cindy stayed at the bar. A man in his mid-20s wearing a cowboy hat approached her.

"Let's you and me get out of here," he said to Cindy.

"Forget it," said Cindy.

"Nah, you got nothing better to do," he said.

"Look, I'm married."

"That don't matter," he said.

Charboneau saw that Cindy was upset. He walked over to the man with the cowboy hat.

"Why don't you take a hike," Joe said to him.

"Free country, I don't have to go anywhere," replied the man.

Joe gently knocked the hat off the man's head. The cowboy was startled, but not nearly as surprised as when one of Joe's teammates strolled over and punched him in the jaw. Immediately, two more of Joe's friends came to stand beside Cindy.

What Joe and his three friends did not realize was that the cowboy had about ten of his compatriots in the bar. Suddenly, bodies began flying over the bar. Bottles and cans filled the air. Two men picked up Joe and pinned him into the corner. Cindy went to the other side of the room to be out of the way yet still able to watch. The two guys were working Joe over with body punches. They seemed ready to bang his head against the wall, when one of his hands broke free. He grabbed a beer mug and smashed it directly into the face of one of his adversaries. In the same motion, he kneed the other one in the stomach. Both men went down.

Just as Joe stepped forward, he was pushed on top of a pool table. He found a pool cue and began swinging. He stood up on the table and belted people with the cue stick. Two more cowboys went down. Then Joe spotted another cowboy trying to sneak out the back door. He leaped at the man, bringing him to the floor, and then he knocked him out.

"The whole thing probably took ten minutes," said Joe. "It was a classic barroom brawl, just like they have in the Western movies."

"It was incredible," said Cindy. "That was the first and only time I had ever seen Joe in a fight, and he knocked out four guys. Joe and his three friends cleaned that place out."

When the fight ended, the floor was a sea of broken glass, cans and bodies. The bartender told Joe to depart immediately. He had called the police.

"He said that he didn't want us to get in trouble," said Joe. "He said that those guys had been asking for someone to beat the hell out of them for a long time. Really, those cowboys loved it. They were just a bunch of rednecks whose idea of a good time was to go out, kick some ass and get knocked around."

The Joe Charboneau stories from that year at Visalia seem endless. But the one tale which is the most infamous is enough to make your stomach rumble and squirm.

Joe visited the dentist and learned that one of his back teeth needed a root canal job. The price would be $250. He was only clearing $500 a month and did not feel like spending half of that amount on his mouth. Then again, Joe saw nothing extravagant about putting out $100 for an alligator and its tank.

"My tooth hurt, that's all I knew," said Joe. "I told the guy just to pull it and not to worry. He said that they try to save a tooth whenever possible. I didn't think any one of my teeth was worth $250."

So Charboneau decided to do what the dentist would not. His methods were straight out of the King Kong school of dentistry. The motto of this school is, "When all else fails, rip it out."

With this in mind, Joe purchased a razor blade, a vise grip, pliers and a fifth of whiskey.

"The first thing I did was drink about half the whiskey," said Joe. "That was a mistake because I don't particularly like whiskey, and it bothered my stomach. Then I cut into the gum around the tooth with a razor. Next, I put the vise grip around it and loosened it. Finally, I yanked it out with the pliers and finished off the whiskey, rubbing a lot of it on my gums."

"I didn't know about his pulling the tooth," said Cindy. "If I had, I would have made him go to the dentist."

A week later, Joe was still feeling the effects of his expedition into his mouth.

"My stomach really acted up on me," said Joe. "But that was because of the whiskey more than anything else. I could never drink whiskey."

Life on the road in the Minors consists of soap-opera-watching afternoons, games before a small circle of friends at night and supper at McDonalds. Of course there are variations, but the key word in this scheme is "monotony."

"With $6.50-a-day meal money, you didn't have enough to eat on, much less go to a bar," said Joe. "The big thing to do was to go out and buy a couple of sixpacks and bags of pistachio nuts. You'd drink and eat and watch the late movie until you fell asleep. When you woke up, you'd hurt your feet on the shells you threw on the floor."

As one would expect, Charboneau did find a way to break out of the rut.

"I remember our first trip into Reno," said Joe. "I had never gambled before. The same was true of some of the other guys on the team. In the back of the bus, we were sitting around and singing 'I got the gambling fever' over and over again. We were on a four-day trip to Reno and they gave us our meal money in advance. I got $26. When we got there, the first thing we did was hit the casinos. I hung around with this other player, who said he was a blackjack expert. He talked me into giving him all my money as a stake. An hour later, he had lost everything."

Facing three penniless days in Reno, Joe called Cindy and described his plight. She decided that Joe deserved another shot at the tables, and $50 was dispatched to him.

"This time, I did all my own gambling," said Joe. "I lost the $50 in the next three days."

But it was a trip to Lodi that almost brought a premature conclusion to Joe's comeback.

"We got rained out. This other player and I were bored," said Joe. "We had stopped at a 7 & 11 store, bought a couple of six-packs and finished them off. We were staying in this dive. It was a great place to put a baseball team. There wasn't a place within five miles to get something to eat."

Charboneau and his teammate discussed their dilemma. They were more than a little drunk, and ravenously hungry. Outside the rain pelted the windows.

"Hell, let's walk to the restaurant," said Joe.

They stepped out the door and began their journey. After 100 yards, it was clear that this was a stupid plan. They were soaked and weaving around on the sidewalk.

"Let's get a car," said Joe.

"Good idea," said Charboneau's teammate.

They went over to a used-car lot and found a 1967 Mustang. The keys were in the ignition, and the door was open. Joe went in the passenger side, and his friend slipped behind the wheel. He floored it out of the lot, and they broke through the chain which served as a gate. They were talking about what a great move they had made when Joe noticed something wrong.

"Hey, we're on a one-way street," said Joe.

"So what," said the friend.

"So we're going the wrong way."

They made a U-turn and spotted flashing red lights behind them. Visions of doing 10 to 20 years zoomed through Joe's mind. He knew that he had often walked the legal tightrope, going back to his boxcar fighting days. This time, he was sure he had fallen off the wire. He wasn't even thinking about his baseball career. He was just hoping to stay out of jail.

"Let's make a run for it," said Joe.

"We're gonna outrun the cops in a 1967 Mustang? No way," said Joe's teammate. "I'm pulling over."

Joe's friend got out of the car and approached the policeman.

"Officer, we are ballplayers from the Visalia Oaks," he said. "We were supposed to play Lodi, but we were rained out. We drove here and were looking for a place to eat and then got lost."

"Let's see your license," the policeman said.

He checked the license and said, "Okay, go ahead, but be more careful next time."

As Joe's friend returned to the car, Joe said, "Let's put this thing back right now."

They drove the car back to its original spot in the parking lot. Joe took a lace from his shoe and tied the chain gate back to the post. His heart was pounding in his chest. He felt like it would burst through at any moment. He began running back to the hotel. Suddenly, he found himself sprinting through a nursery, with his laceless shoe flopping. He stepped into a hole and tripped. He literally flew up in the air and landed face first in a small pond. He pulled himself up and staggered back to his room.

"The thing that made the Minors fun was the people," said Joe. "None of us had any money, and we all wanted the same thing—to get to the Majors. We did a lot of crazy stuff like the thing with the car, but it is the people I remember the most."

One of Joe's teammates in the Philadelphia system was an outfielder who said he was from Las Vegas. He was a constant borrower of money, even though he claimed to own a private jet. He was the kind of guy who would lie on the hood of a car to get a suntan.

"He was something out of 'Sha Na Na,'" said Joe. "He always wore sunglasses which hid his eyes. He liked leather clothes and greased hair. During games, he would roll up his sleeves as far as they could go so he could get a tan. A lot of weird things kept happening to him. In one year, he got the crabs, pyorrhea, the clap, and was bitten by a spider."

On the field, Joe's average fluctuated between .390 and .326. His low point came at the end of a 1-for-52 slump.

"I was in a three-way tie for the batting title on the last day of the season," said Joe. "Tim Flannery, Mike Wilson and I were all hitting .349." Wilson went 1-for-4, Flannery was 1-for-3 and I was 2-for-3 to end up at .3501 with Flannery at .3500."

This was a year of vindication for Joe. He proved that he could hit when given the opportunity.

"All Joe needed was to get away from the Phillies," said Frank Lucy. "That relaxed him. In Visalia, they left him alone and let him be himself, and he hit great."

A sidelight to the 1978 season was that Visalia's batting practice pitcher was a Minnesota scout named Lee Irwin. He was the same Lee Irwin who had been tossed out of Joe's house after downgrading Charboneau's talent.

"We said very little to each other," said Joe. "He apologized for the way he had acted, and I told him not to worry about it."

As for Potatohead Henry, the man who lost his job to Charboneau, he finished the year with a .216 batting average and five homers. He was not one of the California League's honor graduates.

Players from the 1978 California League who have played in the Majors include Charboneau with Cleveland, Flannery with San Diego, Max Venable with San Francisco and Mike Bread with Oakland.

As the 1978 season came to a close, Joe became extremely aware of the price paid by all Minor League players. To play Minor League baseball at a salary of $750 a month for the five months of the season is financial disaster.

"I never had more than $20 in my wallet at one time," said Joe. "After my year at Visalia, we were probably $10,000 in debt to relatives. I didn't own a suit. Actually, I had one, but the coat was too small and the pants were too big. I got it from the Salvation Army Store."

"We were very happy," said Cindy. "Joe and I never had much money from the beginning of our marriage, so we didn't miss having things. It was great. We seldom argued. The one fight I do remember was after a party at our place. It was 3 A.M. He wanted me to make him some pancakes. I had gone to bed, and when he woke me up, I told him to make his own pancakes. So he went into the kitchen and poured some pancake batter and flour on the floor. Then he poured syrup over everything. Needless to say, I wasn't thrilled, and he cleaned it up the next morning."

10 ★★★★★★

THE DEAL

After Joe's productive summer at Visalia, the Phillies welcomed him home like some prodigal son. It is amazing what a .350 batting average will do. Suddenly, you're not such a bad guy.

Philadelphia invited him to its Instructional League program, which runs from October to the end of November. It is a showcase for a club's top young talent. Joe and Cindy moved to Clearwater, Florida, where they rented an apartment on the beach. Cindy was about two months pregnant, and Joe's career was blossoming. This was a good time, a time of hopes and a time of perpetual smiles. The only bit of reality that crept into the situation was Cindy's pregnancy, which had forced her into bed for the first two weeks of the winter program. For Joe, this was a vindication. The Phillies had tried to bury him. They had benched him. They had let him sit at home. They had sent him to another Minor League organization. Now, they brought him together with the likes of Dickie Noles, Keith Moreland and Marty Bystrom—players who would be a part of the Phillies in the 1980s.

The Winter Instructional League has been called "a false spring" by former Minor League pitcher (turned author) Pat Jordan. Jordon's point is that the program is run like spring training. There are games, but only a few retirees show up. In the mornings, the players all work out under a plethora of coaches. The Phillies had name instructors for 25 players. You'd see a pitcher throwing to a hitter, while a coach stood behind the mound, arms folded, whispering in a smooth comforting voice to the hurler before each pitch. In the afternoon, there are games against other Instructional League clubs. These are almost glorified pickup games. There is no pressure, no attention paid to the score. A pitcher may throw 50 percent changeups, as he tries to master that one pitch. A hitter will try to hit everything to rightfield, learning that offensive maneuver. The audience is composed of scouts and coaches. The atmosphere is positive, like that of a high school honors class. The accent is on the future, the stardom and money to come and the eventual arrival in the Major Leagues.

"The thing about the Phillies was that they were overstaffed," said Charboneau. "They had nine guys running around telling you things. One coach would say that you should do something this way, and then another would say you should do it a different way."

Philadelphia was still not in love with Joe. The coaches still winced at the way his cap sat on top of his head, instead of being pulled down over his eyes like most of the other players' caps. Joe was also fined for having his baseball socks too high and for pulling stunts like eating crackers on the field during workouts. It was a buck here, two dollars there. The Phillies were doing what they could to jam Charboneau into their staid system.

At night, the young Phillies were left to their own devices. This meant a lot of time spent on the beach guzzling beer bought from the Little General Food Mart.

"I remember Halloween Night," said Joe. "A bunch of us bought a couple dozen eggs and went out throwing them at cars. Later that evening, Dickie Noles along with Cindy and I were sitting in our apartment. Suddenly, this guy busts through the door. His face was red. Some guys had egged his Mercedes. Noles walked right up to him. They were nose-to-nose. Dickie is a tough guy, and when he gets mad, he gets this strange and scary look in his eyes. The guy looked at Noles and walked out."

After spending two weeks confined to the apartment because of the effects of her pregnancy, Cindy wanted to go to the beach. It was too much, too soon. All the movement made Cindy feel far worse than ever before. Joe rushed her back to the apartment. He took her into the bathroom, where she lost their child.

"We were heartsick," said Cindy. "We wanted that baby so badly. I was down for a long time. It was more a mental than a physical thing. We both sort of moped around after it happened."

While Joe was playing in the Instructional League, the scouts were watching very closely. One who could not keep his eyes off Joe was Dan Carnevale of the Cleveland Indians.

"I remember seeing Joe in this game against our Instructional League team," said Carnevale. "He hit four shots. One of them went about 400 feet over the fence. Another was hit about 400 feet again, this one off the wall. There was something special about the way the ball left his bat."

Carnevale made a note and sent it to his boss, Cleveland Minor League Director, Bob Quinn. This was the first step in making Joe Charboneau an Indian.

"As the Instructional League was ending, I got a call from the Phillies," said Quinn. "They were interested in a Minor League pitcher we had named Cardell Camper. They wanted to talk about him at the winter baseball meetings."

The winter baseball meetings are held in the first week of December each year. They are a baseball convention. There are parties and seminars. Everyone from Commissioner Bowie Kuhn to the general manager of baseball's smallest Minor League city, Paintsville, Kentucky, attend. Executives meet in bars and lobby corners. They talk trades, write names on napkins and check their baseball registers for information on another club's players.

In December of 1978, Cardell Camper was 26. He was a right-hander who had spent three years in Class AAA and had lost more games than he had won.

Bob Quinn was not the only man looking forward to the winter meetings.

"All players know what happens at the meetings," said Joe. "I was hoping that I would get drafted from the Phillies by another team."

Philadelphia had placed Charboneau on its Class AAA roster. This meant a Major League club could draft him from the Phillies for $25,000. If they did, they would have to keep Joe on the big league roster for the first 90 days of the season. The Phillies were well aware that no team would take a player out of Class A, like Joe, and put him in the Majors. That is why they were not concerned about Joe's eligibility for the draft.

Charboneau had other feelings, however.

"After hitting so well at Visalia, I believed that I was ready for the Majors," said Joe. "I saw no need for me to play in the Minors any more."

"There was no way we were going to draft Joe," said Quinn. "We liked him, but it takes a super, super player to make the jump from Visalia to the Majors. We thought Joe was good and thought he had great potential, but no way did we think he could play in the Majors in 1979."

"When the draft came and went, I was depressed," said Joe. "Especially when I heard that Max Venable was picked and I wasn't."

Venable played against Joe in the California League. He was a member of the Lodi Dodgers and he batted .318, 32 points less than Charboneau.

After the 1978 Instructional League season, Joe was loading trucks for $3.75 an hour at the TOYS-R-US warehouse. Often times he worked 14 hours a day.

"I remember coming home after the day of the Minor League draft," said Joe. "I was dead tired, and then I heard that I didn't get drafted and Venable did. I couldn't believe that a team like Seattle or Toronto wouldn't take a chance on me."

While Charboneau was adding more bulk to his frame, by lifting crates of Christmas toys, Bob Quinn and Philadelphia Minor League Director Howie Bedell were talking at the winter meetings in Orlando, Florida.

After first hearing of Charboneau from Carnevale, Quinn checked a report on Joe by the Major League Scouting Bureau. The scouting bureau is a service most Major League clubs purchase. They receive computer printouts rating every amateur and Minor League baseball player of consequence. A scout named Buddy Peterson had watched Charboneau during his awesome season at Visalia. Peterson's report characterized Joe as a "Class AA player at best. He has a big loop swing and has trouble with slow stuff. His arm is way below average, and he doesn't put out 100 percent. He is not a Major League prospect." You could say that 1978 was not a good year for Peterson. In addition to underrating Joe, he also turned in this report on current San Diego Padres second baseman Tim Flannery. Flannery batted .3500 in the California League and lost the batting title on the last day to Charboneau, who hit .3501. Peterson said that "Flannery was a Class A player at best. He has limited range and a slow bat."

"When our scout says something different than the Bureau, we always take the word of our own scouts," said Quinn. "That is why the Scouting Bureau's report did not bother us. Carnevale said that Joe had Major League power, and so we set out to get him."

There is a certain strategy when it comes to trading. Like all baseball executives, Quinn is well-versed in these nuances, and he enjoys the verbal sparring.

"After we learned of Philadelphia's interest in Camper, I sat down with Carnevale, and he made a list of six players from the Phillies Instructional League we would like to have."

Charboneau was one of those names. The others were Dickie Noles, Keith Moreland, Marty Bystrom along with two pitchers named Scott Munninghoff and Henry Mack.

"The guy we really wanted was Charboneau," said Quinn. "But I knew that we needed some pitching. I didn't think the Phillies would be willing to give up any of those other guys, but I asked them."

Quinn and Bedell were old friends. Bedell played for Quinn when Bob was the general manager of the Reading Phillies in 1967–68. Quinn asked for Munninghoff or Bystrom in exchange for Camper. Bedell said no way. Next, he tried for Noles or Mack. Then came Charboneau or Moreland. The first exchanging of names took place on Monday.

"By Wednesday night, I told Bedell that we would trade Camper for Charboneau," said Quinn. "We were on the way to a banquet, and I told him that I needed an answer by the end of the banquet."

Quinn felt that he could heist Charboneau because he knew that the Phillies were not exactly enthralled with his attitude. He had heard of Joe's antics, of his leaving games before their conclusion in 1977 and later his hiatus from the game.

"I wasn't that apprehensive about Joe," said Quinn. "It is like (Indians General Manager) Phil Seghi always tells me, 'If you want good guys, you can stand in front of a church on Sunday morning and sign people.' People kept telling us that Dave Winfield was a bad guy when he was at the University of Minnesota. All he did was jump straight from college to the Major Leagues and then become a favorite in the San Diego community by buying a bunch of baseball tickets for underprivileged kids so they could go to Padres games."

By the end of the banquet, Howie Bedell had agreed to trade Charboneau for Camper. Now, Quinn, along with Phil Seghi, had to get final approval for the trade from Indians President Gabe Paul. While Quinn has indicated that there was little trouble convincing Paul of the merits of the Charboneau deal, other sources reveal that the Indians President was not so sure of the transaction.

"Quinn and Phil Seghi had to argue like hell with Paul about it," said one source. "Gabe does not like to trade pitching. He really liked Camper. He thought the guy had a shot at pitching in the Majors."

In the end, Paul consented, and the deal was consummated.

Charboneau did not learn of the trade until the next day.

"Cindy and I were living with my mother," recalled Joe. "We had gone out Christmas shopping. When we came home, my brother had a message for me to call a guy named 'Howie Biddle' from the Phillies. I knew that John meant Howie Bedell. John said that Bedell had told him that I had been traded."

So Charboneau returned Bedell's call.

"We've traded you to Cleveland," Bedell told him.

"For whom?" asked Joe.

"Cardell Camper."

"Oh," said Joe.

When Joe hung up, he started jumping up and down.

"I was so happy to get away from the Phillies," said Joe. "I had never heard of Cardell Camper, and I had never been to Cleveland, but I knew it was a break for me just to go to another organization that wanted me enough to trade for me. I knew that Cleveland hadn't done that well, and I figured I could help them."

Shortly after talking to Bedell, Joe's phone rang again. This time, it was Bob Quinn calling him.

"He welcomed me to the Indians," said Joe. "Then he said that he hoped I would not quit again."

In that conversation, Joe also agreed to a contract. He would receive $1,000 a month if he played Class AA and $1,100 for Class AAA.

"The credit for the deal must go to Dan Carnevale," said Quinn. "He saw Joe play about six times and really liked him. He said that Joe had this great power, but he only struck out half as much as most power hitters. He said we had to get him."

"I was lucky, to an extent, because I hurt my wrist during the Instructional League and did not play that much," said Charboneau. "But I was healthy when we played Cleveland, and I had my best days. I guess that is why they traded for me."

And whatever became of Cardell Camper? In 1979, he went 7-7 for the Phillies Class AA Reading club. He was released by them in the spring of 1980 and called Bob Quinn last summer, asking for a chance to sign with the Indians. At 28, the Indians felt he was too old, and the career of Cardell Camper will go down as a footnote in baseball history. He is like Roger Alexander and Dave May, who were traded for Hank Aaron. Cardell Camper will live on as the man traded for Super Joe Charboneau.

11 ★★★★★★★★

CHATTANOOGA

Being traded to a new team is like transferring to a new school. There is worry, apprehension and the fear of not being accepted. Charboneau did not like the Phillies organization, but at least he knew them. He could tell when they would chastise or praise him. There is some solace in knowing what will happen next, even if things probably won't turn out very well. Uncertainty is the scariest thing of all.

"With the Indians I didn't know what to expect," said Joe. "I thought that the players might not like me. I got along great with the guys in the Phillies system and later with the guys at Visalia. I enjoyed those people, and I didn't like the thought of leaving them, even though I knew instantly that the trade was the best thing that ever happened to me."

In mid-March, Joe departed for the Cleveland Indians' spring training camp in Tucson, Arizona. He was to work out with the Tribe's Class AAA Tacoma club, which began its drills about a month after the Cleveland players reported to camp. Most Minor League clubs do not hold their initial practices until a month after big league camp opens. This is a cost saving device, since Major League clubs like to avoid paying the expenses of over 100 Minor Leaguers' for as long as possible. In Tucson, Joe received $100-a-week meal money and free board at a motel. It is interesting to note that the Major League teams feel they need six to seven weeks to prepare for the season, while the Minor Leaguers are expected to be ready in three to four weeks.

Joe's first day as a member of the Cleveland organization confirmed all his anxieties.

"The Indians sent a car to pick me up at the airport," recalled Joe. "There were three other players in the car, and none of them said a word to me as we rode to the Spanish Trail Hotel. I wondered what was going on, or if something was wrong. I thought that maybe these guys weren't going to talk to me because they had heard I had a bad reputation or something."

An individual especially susceptible to the pangs of loneliness, Joe felt like an island during that first day in Tucson. No roommate had been assigned to him yet, and Cindy had remained in Santa Clara.

"I was looking for anything that would kill the time," said Joe. "First, I walked to McDonalds and got something to eat. Then I went to Dunkin' Doughnuts. Finally, I bought a six-pack from a 7 & 11 store and went back to my room."

The following day, Joe received not one, but two roommates. Mike Elliott and Jack DuBeau were two of five players who would share a room with Charboneau that spring, and all five of those players would eventually be released.

"Elliott and DuBeau were with me the longest," said Joe. "We got along great. We had a nerf basketball court set up, and we used to play a lot and beat the hell out of each other. Elliott was a diabetic, and I always wanted to give him his insulin shot. We had a lot of good times just sitting around talking and drinking beer."

Despite his pleasure at finally being rid of the Phillies, Joe was upset that the Indians did not invite him to train with the big leaguers. "I hit .350," explained Joe, who was oblivious to the fact that the number of Class A players asked to work out with the Big Club is less than the number of hairs on the head of Telly Savalas.

Joe was off to a fast start with the Tacoma club. He batted .400 that spring with six home runs.

"I thought I would play Class AAA in Tacoma for sure," said Joe.

"I was hitting in the middle of the lineup, and I was doing really well. Then the front office made some moves, and I knew I was in trouble."

In the waning days of the spring, the Tribe acquired outfielders Dell Alston, Sheldon Mallory and Rich Chiles. All three players had extensive Class AAA experience, in addition to being in the Majors long enough to make a few road trips.

Minor Leaguers live in fear of front office maneuvers such as these. They know that a player brought in from another organization almost always receives an excellent chance to display his skills at the highest possible level. After all, a team traded for him, so it would make little sense for that club not to discover what the new athlete could do.

Major League organizations operate under the trickle down theory. Any change at the upper echelons sends shock waves through the rest of the organization. For example, when a Class AAA catcher is promoted to the Majors, odds are that the Class AA catcher will move up to Class AAA and the Class A catcher will go to Class AA. The same process works in reverse when a Major Leaguer is sent down to Class AAA.

In the spring, many players exist on the dangerous periphery of the game. They are a part of the system. They are pros, ballplayers paid to perform. But if their skills are marginal, they know that they are always close to the final chapters of their careers. Minor Leaguers pray that their stay in the game won't be a short story, but for many that is the case. Only 10 percent of all players signed eventually wear a Major League uniform. Less than five percent are still active at age 30.

Joe's roommates knew all about this delicate position. Mike Elliott, Jack DuBeau and three others, who would eventually take a place in Charboneau's room, all fretted, spending restless nights wondering if they would hear those six awful words which echoed throughout the Indians Minor League camp near the end of spring training. The six words were, "Bob Quinn wants to see you." That was it, the obituary. Quinn would ache, and his stomach would rebel and sicken him as he told a prospect that he was through and that he would not be one of those 10-percenters who beat the odds.

"After Elliott and DuBeau got cut, I kept getting roommates for a couple of days, and then they would be released," said Charboneau.

"My place was like a revolving door. People were wondering if I was some sort of jinx."

Fortunately, Charboneau did not concern himself with the possibility of the axe catching up with him. Even though the Indians started the spring with about 35 more players in camp than jobs available, Joe knew he would survive and eventually thrive. Not everything was perfect, however.

When the Indians obtained Mallory, Alston and Chiles, the front office saw no need for Charboneau to make the huge leap from Class A (where he played at Visalia) to Class AAA. Even though he had had a very successful spring, the Tribe did not want to rush him.

"I was on the bus with the Tacoma team. We were going to play the Oakland A's Major League club in an exhibition game in Scottsdale. I was really looking forward to going."

As Joe sat on the bus awaiting its departure, Tacoma Manager Gene Dusan walked up to him.

"Joe, you're not going with us," said Dusan.

That was it. Joe immediately realized the ramifications of that small phrase. Not only would he not make the trip, he would not play in Tacoma. Instead of playing in the Pacific Coast League, where the team traveled by airplane and received $12.50-a-day meal money, he was headed to Chattanooga of the Southern League, where the mode of transportation was the bus and meal money was $8.50. Being cut also meant he would earn $1,000 a month, instead of $1,100 if he had stuck in Class AAA, under the terms of his split contract.

And so it was; life was not too bad for Joe Charboneau. Not bad at all. While not thrilled about being sent to Chattanooga, his disappointment at failing to make Class AAA was brief.

Joe was feeling good about himself, his wife and his career. First of all, Cindy had joined Joe in Chattanooga, and she was pregnant once again. Secondly, Joe was the Lookouts' cleanup batter, and he had tripled and knocked in two runs in Chattanooga's 3-2 opening day loss to Charlotte. Finally, he felt an affinity for the Indians.

"We wanted Joe to know that we liked him and cared what happened to him and his wife," said Bob Quinn. "It sounds trite, but we wanted him to feel that he was a part of the Indians' family."

A baseball organization far more resembles a college fraternity than a nuclear family. Members of your family are never cut. Because of the game's liquid nature, players come and go. They are hurt, traded, released or they quit. But strong friendships do form, and it is possible for a player to have an extremely positive opinion of the Major League organization that employs him. Joe felt that way about the Indians. They were the first team to tell him that he would one day play in the Majors, and that he could be a star. "Bob Quinn would always talk to me, and he gave me a lot of confidence," said Joe. "He wouldn't let me get down, and I knew he wanted me to make it. He was pulling for me."

Charboneau started quickly at Chattanooga and was hitting .400 at the end of the season's first month. He and Cindy shared a two-bedroom apartment with teammates Vic Holmstedt and Robin Fuson. During the baseball year, the Charboneaus would never live alone until Joe became a member of the Cleveland Indians.

"I was very happy with the way things were going," said Joe. "Scouts and some coaches told me that I would be lucky to hit .290 in the Southern League. They said it was the toughest league to hit in of all the Minor Leagues. In the spring, I told one of my teammates to tell a Chattanooga reporter that I would win the batting title and hit .350. I knew it sounded like bragging, but I believed I could do it."

The Southern League is a dirty word to most men who spend their lives beating the bushes. The league is set up as if it were designed for the greater glory and profits of the Greyhound Bus Company. The cities are spread from Nashville, Tennessee, to Orlando, Florida to Montgomery, Alabama. In between, there are Savannah, Memphis, Knoxville, Charlotte, Columbus (Georgia) and Jacksonville. The Lookouts' (Chattanooga) longest trek is 550 miles to Orlando and the shortest is 112 miles to Knoxville. And what about flying? That's for the birds, but not Southern Leaguers.

"I have played and managed in nine different Minor Leagues," said Atlanta Braves coach Bobby Dews. "And none of them compare with

the Southern League in terms of fatigue and awful travel. They say the
Southern League is like boot camp. If you can cut it there, you will
make it anywhere."

For Southern League players, the bus is their second home. They
eat, sleep, read, talk, drink, write letters, go to the bathroom and even
change clothes on the bus. The schedule is composed so that there are
no off days (with the exception of the All-Star break) between the
start of the season in mid-April and its early September conclusion.

This means that you leave a town like Chattanooga after a night
game and ride 12 hours to a place like Orlando, arriving at the hotel
about 10 A.M. There are usually no stops. Most players do not know
whether to eat or sleep when they finally get off the bus. The only
thing they are certain of is that they hate that bus more than anything
or anyone they have ever encountered. Those maddening trips make
them weak in the mind and knees. They walk off the bus dirty and
stinking of sweat and the other by-products of sleeping in your
clothes.

What makes all this worse is the climate of the South. During the
day, the temperature is between 95 and 100 degrees. At night, it "cools
off" to 90. You sweat when you sit, and moving causes a veritable
flood of perspiration. Southern League players do not know what it
means not to have a sweat-soaked uniform sticking to their bodies.
They think, "So this is what it means to be a pro," and they wonder if it
is worth it. This is an interstate league, with the players learning every
inch and road sign of I-95, I-75, I-85 and I-76. They sleep in Days Inns
and Holiday Inns and eat at Sambo's and Denny's.

"I could never sleep on a bus," said Joe. "That's a major disadvan-
tage, especially in the Southern League. I would try. Some guys would
sleep on the overhead luggage compartments or across two seats. I
would sprawl out on the floor in the back. That way my muscles
wouldn't tighten, but I would get soaked with the beer that spilled on
the floor, along with getting filthy. It is some way to live."

There were good times on the bus, however. Once, Joe and his road
roommate, Dave Riveria, managed to bring a keg of beer on the bus
without the knowledge of Lookouts Manager Woody Smith. That

made the ride much more pleasant and much shorter. It also produced a hung-over baseball team the following day.

"At least three or four guys passed-out on that trip," said Joe. "They would come to the back of the bus and say, 'We're gonna drink with you and Riveria.' After a couple beers, they were done."

Riveria and Charboneau became very close that season.

"One night we were staying in Montgomery," said Joe. "It was a really lousy neighborhood. It was June 17, my birthday, and I was hitting .404. Riveria said that we should celebrate. There were no bars around. Dave told me to call Cindy, and he went out for a walk. About a half-hour later, he came back with a case of beer. He had bought it from an Alabama bootlegger, and it cost him $30. Riveria is a great guy. He has to be to do something like that."

A guy with a .400 batting average, a huge fluffy Afro sticking out from under his cap and a volatile temper is bound to attract attention and followers. In Chattanooga, they called Charboneau, "Jo-Jo." Those small but loyal audiences at Lookout games cheered and worshipped him like any group of fans who have just discovered a new hero.

"Joe was big in Chattanooga," said Cindy. "I filled a scrapbook with all the newspaper stories. It was the first time he received a lot of print."

Charboneau's actions with umpires also had several people watching him closely. One was Southern League President Billy Hitchcock, who continually received bizarre reports about Joe's conduct on the field, especially with umpires. They included the following:

* In one game, Joe did not like a called strike by the home plate umpire. He was jowl-to-jowl with the umpire, as both parties screamed about the decision. Chattanooga Manager Woody Smith broke in between Charboneau and the umpire. He wanted to protect his player. Joe would have none of it. He picked up the 205-pound Smith and placed him off to the side so he could continue the argument himself. "It was the damnedest thing I ever saw," said Bob Quinn, who was visiting Chattanooga that day. "He lifted Woody, who is built like a heavy fireplug, and moved him like he was a baby."

* Another game saw Joe become enraged at an umpire's decision. Rather than dispute the call on the field, he returned to the dugout and tossed every bat out of the rack onto the diamond. One at a time. Then he kicked the watercooler unmercifully.

* A third incident occurred when Joe grounded out to end an inning. Disgusted, he grabbed the batting helmet off his head and blindly flung it. It hit the top of the Chattanooga dugout and bounced into the grandstand, striking a lady in the face.

"I was really worried that I had hurt her," said Joe. "But she was just stunned. I gave her a baseball and apologized. She was very good about everything We had great fans at Chattanooga. I remember one game where Vic Holmstedt went out and pitched, right after learning that his father had died. A couple of fans found out about it, and they took up a collection from the rest of the crowd to pay for Vic's airfare back to the West Coast for the funeral."

* The incident which made Joe a Southern League legend had nothing to do with umpires.

Bill Gullickson was pitching for Memphis. Now a member of the Montreal Expos who fanned 18 batters in one Major League game, Gullickson was known for his awesome fastball.

"Gullickson had just been sent down from Class AAA," said Charboneau. "You could tell that he was pissed off at the world. He was pitching the second game of a doubleheader. In the opener I had hit a grand slam. I heard that he had it in for me."

Before stepping into the batter's box, Joe goes through a ritual consisting of three full swings, ten strokes of his foot to wipe away the lines in the batter's box along with tightening his batting gloves.

"Hurry up, hot dog," Gullickson screamed at him from the mound.

The count ran to three balls and a strike. Then Joe swung and missed a pitch and ended up falling down.

"Nice swing, jerk," Gullickson yelled at him.

Joe charged the mound. He and Gullickson stood a few inches apart glaring at each other. Then Joe returned to home plate. Gullickson delivered an outside fastball, and Charboneau hit it over the rightfield wall for a home run. Charboneau began a ridiculously slow home run trot. He stopped at first base and shouted, "Nice pitch, jerk," to Gullickson.

As Joe reached second base, Gullickson gestured maliciously, while Joe continued to scream at him. At third, Joe and the Memphis third baseman exchanged a couple of words and a few shoves.

"It was the longest home run I ever hit," said Joe. "Not because of the distance, but because it took me about five minutes to cover the bases."

The Charboneau-Gullickson feud was far from over. In his next at bat, Gullickson tried to fool Joe with an inside changeup. Charboneau hit it over the leftfield wall for his third homer of the day. At this point, Gullickson was extremely upset, but he was silent and so was Joe.

"I knew he was going to knock me down my next time up," said Joe. "He had to after I had taken his team deep three times."

In his third at bat, Gullickson tossed not one, but two straight pitches behind Joe's head, sending him sprawling both times. But things finally calmed down as Gullickson retired Charboneau on a ground ball.

Billy Hitchcock was growing concerned about Joe Charboneau.

"He fined me $25 for throwing the bats on the field, and he used to send me letters all the time saying that I had to control my temper," said Charboneau. "He came to see me play several times and talked with me. I had pushed an umpire a couple of times, and he said that I had to be cool, and if I did, I would make it to the Majors. He told me that I could not keep doing some of that stuff, and he was right. Hitchcock is a nice man, and he seemed to really care about me. I appreciated him taking the time to talk to me and write me letters, and I didn't mind the reprimands, because I deserved them."

"The thing about Joe was that everybody liked him," said Chattanooga pitcher John Teising. "He had a temper, but he always got mad at himself, unless it was something extreme like the Gullickson incident. What I remember most about Joe is that he loved to kid around. He was always making funny faces and sticking things in his nose to crack people up.

"One of his favorite things was to go out in the bullpen and play the Incredible Hulk," continued Teising. "He would hold this huge rock in front of his chest, and then another guy would ram into him with another rock and break it on Joe's chest. Either that or he would lie down with the rock on him while another guy banged a smaller rock on his chest. When it was over, the rocks would be broken, and Joe would end up full of dust. He loved it."

While Joe was popular with his teammates, he also impressed the league's sportswriters. They voted him to the Southern League All-Star game, which was held in Nashville. The All-Stars played the Atlanta Braves.

"Jim Crittendon was the Chattanooga owner, and he was excited about me going to the All-Star game," said Joe. "He made arrangements for a limousine to pick up Cindy and me at the airport, and take us to the Grand Old Opry Hotel. That was the most expensive and plush place I have ever stayed in. It was even nicer than the places we stayed at the Majors. The great thing about it was that the other players picked for the game stayed at lesser hotels and went to and from the game in vans, while we went in the limo."

The All-Star game was watched by over 10,000 fans, the biggest crowd Joe had ever played before. The Braves were also the first Major League team Joe had faced.

"I was really psyched," said Joe. "I wanted to show everybody that I could hit big leaguers. I was playing so well in Chattanooga that I was surprised I hadn't been called up to Cleveland. I thought if I did something great in the All-Star game that I might get the call to the big show."

Charboneau went 1-for-3 vs. Atlanta. His hit was a two-run double off left-hander Craig Skok, who split the 1979 season between Atlanta and Richmond of the International League. Joe's team defeated the Braves.

After the All-Star game, Charboneau had a few more memorable games, like a night in Nashville when he hit three homers—one to leftfield, then one to rightfield and finally one to center. Mostly, however, the second half was a discouraging time.

"At the end of July, I came down with the mumps," said Joe. "I was in bed for a couple of days with a high temperature."

"Joe went back to play too soon," said Cindy. "He was still sick, but he goes nuts when he doesn't play. In our apartment, he had a batting tee set up, and he would swing his bat and hit a pair of rolled-up socks off of the tee. He hated it when he wasn't in the lineup."

Following his bout with the mumps, Joe was back in the lineup, but immediately pulled a groin muscle running out a ground ball in his first at bat. He sat out for five more days.

"When I went back again I wasn't really ready," said Joe. "My groin still bothered me, but the trainer said that I probably wouldn't suffer any further damage. In baseball, there is always this subtle pressure on you to play, even if you are hurt. Sometimes you can play hurt, and it doesn't have any bad effects."

Charboneau's groin injury was not one of those instances.

"Again I hit a ground ball in my first at bat, and this time I felt like I pulled every muscle in my stomach and groin," said Joe. "The pain was unbearable, and that was it for me for the rest of the year. All I did from there on out was pinch-hit."

While disabled, Charboneau did not use great discretion. Instead of watching his diet, he continued to eat and drink as if he were still playing every day.

"I wasn't being very smart," said Joe. "After games, I would go out and drink beer with the guys. The thing was that I couldn't run it off."

So Joe ballooned. He went from 195 pounds to 205, then to 215 and finally to 220 pounds. That is when Indians General Manager Phil Seghi stopped in Chattanooga to watch the Lookouts.

"He told me that I was getting fat," said Joe. "He said that I had better watch it or I would turn into another Charlie Spikes. I didn't even know who Charlie Spikes was."

Spikes played for the Indians in the middle 1970s. He was a massive, large-boned outfielder who specialized in hitting balls for great distances along with downing equally monstrous quantities of food. His nickname was the "Bogalusa Bomber," after the small Louisiana hamlet where he was raised.

The Indians say that Spikes literally ate his way out of the Majors. As his waistline expanded, his homer total and batting average dropped. Finally, he was traded to the Detroit Tigers for Tom Veryzer. Later, Spikes would disappear from the game, like the food on his plate, for a season, before returning as a spare-part pinch-hitter with the Atlanta Braves. A man who hit 22 homers in his rookie year with Cleveland, Spikes saw his career shrivel with each gulp of mashed potatoes.

Fat or not, Charboneau ended the season with a .352 batting average, along with 21 homers and 78 RBIs. That gave him his second straight Minor League batting title, and he made good on his early-season prediction. Charboneau's average was the highest in the nine-year history of the Southern League, and he won the title by a substantial 25-point margin over Danny Heep of Columbus.

Charboneau would be one of four players who would leap from the Southern League directly to the big leagues in 1980. The others were Chicago White Sox pitchers Britt Burns and Rich Dotson, along with Joe's old adversary Bill Gullickson. Joe also became the second straight American League Rookie of the Year to come from the Southern League. In 1979, Minnesota's John Castino was selected as the League's premier freshman, after spending the 1978 season with Orlando.

While Joe was pleased with the Southern League honors he received, nothing would compare with the thrills he had after the 1979 season.

"We were waiting for our first child to be born," said Joe. "Cindy and I were going to Lamaze classes. She was still a month away when we came home that day and she said that it was time."

Joe ushered Cindy into their car, and they drove to the hospital.

"The doctor said she would have the baby in about two hours," said Joe.

Actually, Cindy spent eight hours in labor. When the child was born, it was a 6-pound 15-ounce boy, who was indeed a month premature. He also had a case of jaundice.

"That was cleared up in a couple of days," said Joe. "We named him Tyson, after this Chattanooga player we knew, Terry Tyson. When he was born it was the happiest day of my life."

12 ★★
★
★
★★★

MEXICO

After the 1979 season came to an end, the scouting reports on Joe Charboneau reflected his statistics for the first time. The Major League Scouting Bureau, which had called him a Class AA player, "at best," just 12 months before, now considered Joe a Major League prospect.

"Charboneau has a compact but powerful swing," said one report. "His arm is still below average, and his speed is ordinary. He's a hothead and doesn't always give 100 percent. A big league hitter."

Bob Quinn saw Charboneau play eight games at Chattanooga and believed that he was ready for the Indians. Quinn spoke with Joe, and it was determined that he was well enough to play winter baseball. The Indians arranged for Joe to travel to Guaymas, Mexico, and test his groin muscle south of the border.

"This was the first time I ever felt like I was making some money from baseball," said Joe. "I was to get $2,000 a month. The Guaymas owner set me up with this apartment right on the ocean. Guaymas is this resort town, and my place was in the tourist section. Places like my apartment usually went for $1,200 a month, but I only had to pay $500."

Guaymas is a city of 55,000 located on the Gulf of California, about

200 miles south of the Arizona border. Getting there was no easy task for Joe.

"I arrived at the San Francisco airport a little early," said Joe. "So I went into the bar for a drink, and the next thing I knew I was in this argument with some guy. I think we were talking about the playoffs. Anyhow, Rodney Craig (of the Seattle Mariners) was going to Guaymas with me. He pulled me out of the bar, and we barely made the flight.

"Everything went okay until we got out of the plane in Guaymas," continued Charboneau. "Then we picked up our bags and baseball equipment and went to the customs inspection. This official looked at me and said he would make me open up everything for this very strict inspection, unless I gave him one of my bats. I had been told that you had to go along to get along in Mexico, so I was glad that he only wanted a bat."

After bribing the customs officials, Joe was taken to his apartment and told that the Guaymas team owner was throwing a party for his players that night.

"We were driven to this castle," said Joe. "I thought it was an office building or something, but it was the owner's house. It was a mansion, the biggest house I had ever seen. They had a bunch of huge steaks and kegs of that dark Mexican beer. I remember getting pretty drunk and bothering some of the Mexican players. Then I remember going back to my place and finding out that I had the worst case of diarrhea ever. I had it the whole time I was in Mexico."

The day after the party, Guaymas played an exhibition game so Manager Bobby Floyd could watch his athletes perform before the regular season began. Floyd had very little time, as Guaymas opened the next day.

"They brought in this team from the countryside to play us," said Joe. "The team was called the Chicken Farmers. That's because they really were chicken farmers. We played on an all-dirt field. I mean the infield, outfield and everything was dirt. The backstop was made of chicken wire, which was no surprise considering our opposition. There were just a couple of wooden bleachers, and all the fans stood down the foul lines. It was like 100 degrees, and I was totally hung over and had to go to the bathroom all the time. I lasted about six innings, and that was it."

There was nothing super about Joe in Mexico. He had ballooned to 230 pounds because of the groin injury, which had led to a large dose of inactivity coupled with an equally large quantity of beer consumption.

"I hit about .210," said Charboneau. "Before every inning I had to run to the bathroom. But the fans seemed to like me, fat and all. They called me Tarzan. Baseball in Mexico is wild. Guards with machine guns walk through the stands. They are there to protect the fans from each other. The fans bet like crazy on the games. They also throw beer on each other and toss around raw eggs.

"But what I remember most about Mexico are the bus trips. We made this twenty-hour one from Guaymas to Tijuana. What are you supposed to do on a bus for twenty hours? We stopped to eat at this place which had a dirt floor. I couldn't believe it. When we got back on the bus, this Mexican player and I got a case of beer. I bet him that I could outdrink him. We headed to the back of the bus and started pouring them down. I tricked the guy, as I poured my beer on the floor when he wasn't looking. I remember that I drank about ten and poured ten out. The guy kept going. He drank twenty beers and then finally passed out. To this day, that Mexican guy thinks I drank twenty beers."

After two weeks in Mexico, Joe reinjured his groin, running out a ground ball to the shortstop.

"They took me to this guy who was supposed to be the best trainer in Mexico. He looked at me and didn't have the slightest idea what to do. Here was the best trainer in Mexico, and he didn't know a damn thing. Finally, he gave me some shot in the groin. I still don't know what kind of shot it was. All I cared about was that he sterilized the needle."

Joe wanted to return to America, since he could no longer play, but an air traffic controllers' strike kept him there for five more days.

"For a while, I walked around the town waiting to get out," said Charboneau. "Guaymas had this really tough section. There were whorehouses, gambling joints and places like that. I remember watching a cockfight. Then one morning this van stopped in front of my apartment. A bunch of soldiers with submachine-guns got out, and they started searching our complex. That's when I went to the owner of the club and told him I had to get out of there.

"He had this guy fly me to Tucson in his private Cessna jet. To this day I don't know if I got out of Mexico legally. Then I ended up spending twenty-two hours in the airport because I was a standby on three straight flights home, and I couldn't get on any of them. I remember sitting in those hard plastic airport chairs, holding all my luggage in my lap so no one would steal it. I even slept that way."

When Joe finally made it back to Santa Clara, he went to live with Cindy, Tyson and his sister Mary.

"I looked like hell," said Joe. "I was fat, I had the runs and my ass was raw. In fact, I was such a blimp that my mother didn't even want to feed me."

During the winter of 1979-80, Joe ate very little. He had been bombarded with letters and telephone calls from the Indians, suggesting that he pull the plug on his blimb-like stomach unless he wanted to make a Southern League curtain call in 1980. Joe thought of the trips from Chattanooga to Orlando and prayed that he would never see the inside of a bus again.

"I knew in my heart that I was ready for the big leagues," said Joe. "I thought so after the 1978 season, and I was convinced of it after '79. Nothing was going to stop me. They wanted me skinny, so I simply didn't eat."

Joe had only two meals a day. There was no sugar, salt or butter. The taste of beer became nothing more than a fond memory. He consumed so much salad and fruit that he wanted to gag at the mention of the word "lettuce."

"The big thing was exercise," said Charboneau. "I worked out every day. I lifted weights. I ran up and down stairs after my groin improved. Every day, I would take Tyson out for an hour-and-a-half walk, and I'd carry him the whole way. He was gaining weight every day."

While Joe was pulling his own version of a Vic Tanny weight loss program, Cindy was working three jobs, hoping to put at least a small dent in their ever-rising debt.

Cindy was employed by Memorex as a tape tester during the day. She would come home for a quick supper and then dash off to McDonalds, where she spent her evenings bagging French fries and serving Big Macs. On weekends, she coached swimming.

"We still weren't getting anywhere financially," said Joe. "I'd say that we were $15,000 in debt at that time. We had $1,200 on our charge card, and they took it away. Most of the money was owed to relatives. We ran up a lot of bills because of the baby. All those clothes and everything are expensive. Just from the money angle, I knew I had to make the Majors pretty soon, or we would never get out from under the bills."

Over the winter, Joe also signed a contract which didn't exactly thrill him. At the time, his agent was San Jose fight promoter Joe Gaglihardi.

"He got me $7,500 if I made Class AAA and $21,000, which is the big league minimum if I stuck with the Indians," said Joe. "I thought I should have received at least $20,000, even if I didn't make the Cleveland team. I figured I deserved that much after the two years I had had in the Minors. But my agent said that I had no leverage and just to go ahead and sign. I was already $1,500 in debt to him, so I went along."

Joe's contract turned out to be worth $30,000 after the Major League players' basic agreement was upgraded in May. Joe paid off Gaglihardi's loan, and they terminated their agreement.

Charboneau kept hearing from the Indians about his weight. He was first urged to drop his weight to 205, then 195, and finally 190.

"I made it to every level they set, and then they told me to lose more," recalled Joe. "Finally, I said, 'I'll lose everything I've got if that's what it takes to make the big show.' We went to spring training on February 15th which was twelve days early. In the morning I went out to the park and ran up and down the bleachers. I took batting practice against the machines, and I was still on the diet. My weight was down to 183, the lightest I have been since I got out of high school."

In retrospect, Joe believes that his crash diet became an obsession. "I did not want an ounce of fat on my body. My waist was a 36 when I started, and I got it down to 31. That winter all I did was train and take care of Tyson, while Cindy supported us. I knew that the scouts had said I always would have trouble with my weight, and I was determined to show the Indians that the scouts were wrong."

This was my first official uniform, when I played little league. "These are the pants with the hole."

Receiving my diploma upon graduation from Buchser High School

My first car—a 1974 Javelin

This is when I signed with the Phillies in 1978

Cindi and I in our living room/before going to spring training with the Phillies

"A happy day." Walking down the aisle with the love of my life

Mom on my wedding
day. She helped make
my dream to play in
the majors come true.

Cindi, myself, and my
mom at the altar after
our wedding. Two peo-
ple who stuck with me
through my career

My son Tyson, myself, and the San Diego Chicken. The Indians' management brought the chicken in for a game against Kansas City. He might have brought me a little luck, as I hit a home run and we won the game.

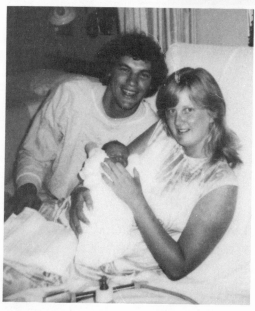

Cindi and myself at the birth of our son, Tyson

My friend and agent Dan and myself at our "engage-
ment," hoping it will lead to a long one.
(Sandy DeGarmo)

Dave Duncan (pitching coach) was always one of the
first to congratulate me after a homer. Dave was my
favorite player when I was growing up in the Oakland
area, and he was playing for the As. *(Janet Macoska/
Kaleyediscope)*

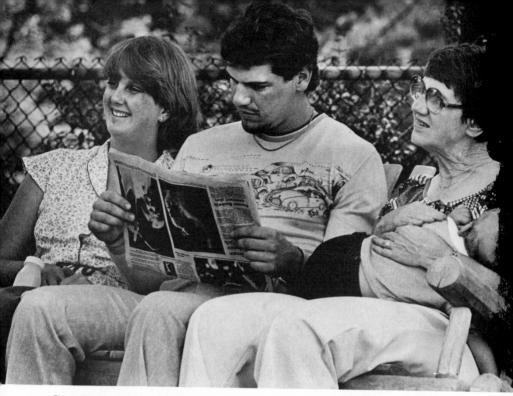

Cindi, myself, my mom, and Tyson in Dan's back yard
during one of my mother's visits to Cleveland

The baseball bug was always tagging along to help entertain the fans before a game. *Janet Macoska/ Kaleyediscope)*

Signing autographs before a game helped to keep me loose, especially with all the support from the fans of Cleveland. *(Janet Macoska/ Kaleyediscope)*

Playing a game is always a team effort, and the Indians were all a great bunch of fellows. *(Paul Tepley)*

Jerry Dybzinski and myself signing autographs. It was the rookie year for both of us, so we related very well together. *(Janet Macoska/-Kaleye-discope)* ▾

The SMACO (Sports Media Association of Cleveland and Ohio) Golf Tournament. "It was Hot."

Ron Hassey, another participant in the SMACO Golf Tournament. Ron, having experienced being a rookie the previous year, really helped me adjust to major league life.

Mike Hargrove was also part of the SMACO Golf Tournament. Mike helped me in more ways than I could begin to thank him for.

Press Star

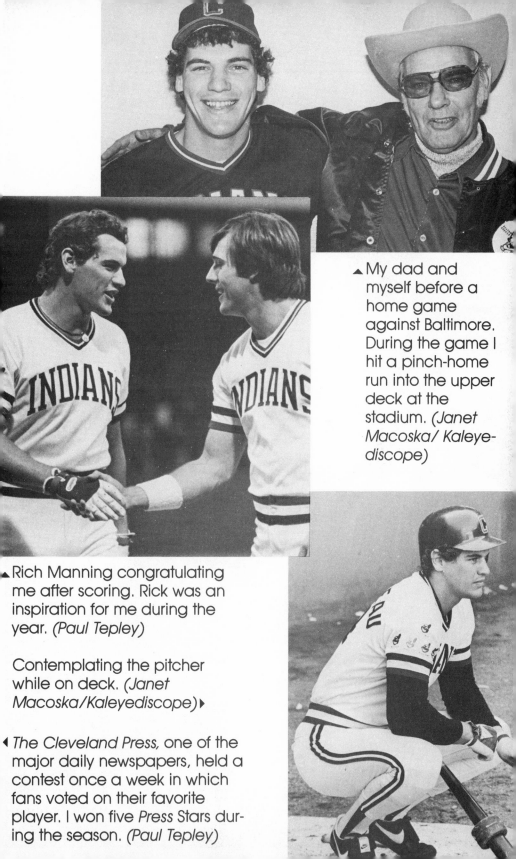

▲ My dad and myself before a home game against Baltimore. During the game I hit a pinch-home run into the upper deck at the stadium. *(Janet Macoska/ Kaleyediscope)*

▲ Rich Manning congratulating me after scoring. Rick was an inspiration for me during the year. *(Paul Tepley)*

Contemplating the pitcher while on deck. *(Janet Macoska/Kaleyediscope)* ▶

◀ *The Cleveland Press,* one of the major daily newspapers, held a contest once a week in which fans voted on their favorite player. I won five *Press* Stars during the season. *(Paul Tepley)*

"Helping other people is the best way to realize your potential, whether it is helping someone who has fallen down on the street or talking to a friend having trouble."

Peter Noone of the Hermans Hermits came to see me before one of my games. *(Janet Macoska/Kaleyediscope)*

The inside of our locker room before a game. All the players relaxed in different ways. *(UPI, Ron Kuntz)*

Contemplating the game. *(Janet Macoska/ Kaleyediscope)*

Talking to the b
"NEED THOSE HI"
(Paul Tepley)

Joe's super fan Don
"Boot" Buttrey.

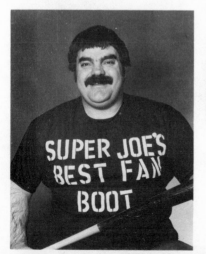

My brother John and myself. John woul
like to be a big league ball player som
day. *(Janet Macoska/Kaleyediscope)*

I keep telling Dan to keep Cindi and Tyson
off my back! *(UPI, Ron Kuntz)*

Doing the World Series analysis as a sports announcer for WMMS Radio Station was a lot of fun.
(Janet Macoska/Kaleyediscope)

My son Tyson and myself. He will always be an everlasting joy in my life. *(Janet Macoska/Kaleyediscope)*

Playing with my son
Tyson *(Paul Tepley)*

A congratulatory kiss from my wife Cindi after being
announced "Rookie of the Year" *(UPI, Ron Kuntz)*

Dan showing me the Heating and Cooling part of his business. Without Dan's support and views on life itself, it would have been hard to make it through the year. Dan always has a bright outlook on life and feels things always happen for a purpose or reason. *(UPI, Ron Kuntz)*

I told Cindi if I started this year I'd win it (Rookie of the Year) for her, which I was fortunate enough to do. *(Janet Macoska/Kaleyediscope)*

Gabe Paul, president of the Cleveland Indians, addressed the media at the presentation of Rookie of the Year. *(Janet Macoska/Kaleyediscope)*

Thanking the media at the Rookie of the Year press conference. *(Janet Macoska/Kaleyediscope)*

Herb Score and myself at the presentation of Rookie of the Year. He was Rookie of the Year in 1955, the year I was born. *(Janet Macoska/Kaleyediscope)*

Phil Seghi, general manager, myself, Gabe Paul, president, and Dan at the signing of my 1981 contract. *(UPI, Ron Kuntz)*

Harrison Dillard (Olympic track star), Mayor George
Voinovich, and myself at the annual Christmas Seals Drive.
(Tibor Gasparik)

Gabe Paul, president, and myself at the signing of my 1981
contract. I hope that it is the first of many with the Cleveland
Indians. (Paul Tepley)

Tom Cousineau and myself. Tom plays football with the Montreal Allouettes and is a close friend of Dan's.I had read about Tom when he played at Ohio State and was thrilled when I met him. *(Janet Macoska/Kaleyediscope)*

Pat Moriarty, Dan, and myself. Pat had played with the Cleveland Browns and is a client of Dan's. I worked out with Pat during the off-season. *(Janet Macoska/Kaleyediscope)*

Jean Nossek and Cindi. Jean helped Cindi quite a bit in coping with being a wife of a major league ballplayer. *(Janet Macoska/Kaleyediscope)*

Joe Nossek, myself, Dan, and Li Miester, a friend of Dan's. Joe was the one who helped me realize the potential I had. *(Janet Macoska/Kaleyediscope)*

Joe admiring Steeler Cliff Stoudt's Super Bowl ring.

Myself, Tyson, Cindi, and Dan Don Donnelly, relaxing at Avon Lakes Country Club before dinner. *(Art Ballant)*

The Big Leagues

13 ★★★★★★

SPRING TRAINING

So this was it. Joseph Charboneau was 24. At times, he felt 34. He knew that time was running out. He was tired of having "a great future." He wanted a present which would be all that he had dreamed.

When Joe prepared to leave his Santa Clara home for the Indians spring training camp in Tucson, he was in a melodramatic mood. He talked about this being his moment, the time he had spent a lifetime working for. "I would never be any more ready to play in the big leagues than I was in the spring of 1980."

Charboneau had quit and come back. In terms of baseball, he was lost and then found. He had smashed pitchers from Lodi to Nashville to Savannah. He was like a play which had received great reviews in Boston and New Haven. There was only one place left to go. Joe was taking his act to baseball's equivalent of Broadway.

"Cindy and I spent the winter looking over the Indians' rosters," recalled Joe. "We watched all the trades and the people placed on the big league roster. We talked about how I had to do something sensational right away to get noticed. We figured I had an outside chance of making the team, but I would need to have a great spring, or they would send me to Class AAA."

Before the spring of 1980, Cleveland baseball fans had read a little about Charboneau.

While snow covered the ground, and Lake Erie was in the midst of
its January freeze, the *Cleveland Plain Dealer* published a Sunday
series of articles dissecting the Tribe's farm system. For the first time
since 1957, all of the Indians Minor League clubs finished with
records above .500. Fifteen prospects were listed, and the man at the
top was Joe Charboneau. Heading into Tucson, he was the designated
phenom. Indian President Gabe Paul said that part of the reason he
was willing to part with enigmatic but productive outfielder Bobby
Bonds for pitching help was that the Indians had Charboneau on
hold.

Joe Charboneau departed from his Santa Clara home February
15th for the Indians' Tucson spring training base.

Like the rest of his career, the road to the Majors would never be
confused with a freeway. This was especially true of Joe's route to the
spring camp.

"It was a fifteen-hour trip, but it ended up taking me twenty-one,"
said Joe. "I had bought Cindy a Datsun pickup over the winter. We
had the thing packed with everything we owned—some pots, pans, a
stereo, records and clothes. As we got around Bakersfield, we hit all
this snow near the mountains. We then took a detour through the
desert around Bishop, California. The ground was flooded. While we
made it through, we had to take it very slowly."

The Indians never look better than they do under the Arizona sun.
It is as if the warmth, the surrounding mountains, the cactus and all
the other ingredients of this idyllic setting are trying to hide the
unhappy fact that John F. Kennedy, Lyndon Johnson, Richard
Nixon, Gerald Ford, Jimmy Carter and Ronald Reagan have all
ascended to the presidency since the Tribe last won a pennant, in 1954.
Excluding expansion teams, every other American League club
except Cleveland has appeared in the World Series since 1954. Cleveland had just finished the 1970s with the second-worst record in the
American League.

Yes, the Tribe had become yet another Cleveland joke, in a city
which had to endure both its major river and its mayor's hair catching
fire, along with innumerable other indignities. The Indians are one of

the reasons people in Cleveland wear T-shirts saying: CLEVELAND, YOU GOTTA BE TOUGH.

Yet hope lingers. The massive Northeast-Ohio sports audience seems to hang much of their faith on the Indians. They seem to feel that if the Indians can pull themselves together, everything else will also fall into place. Of course, the value of a baseball team to a city has often been overstated, but more than one politician has said that nothing makes a populace feel better about itself than a winner on the diamond.

So the fans in Cleveland read their papers in February and March, and say silent prayers that this might be the year that one of those perennial rebuilding jobs actually succeeds. They look at the pictures of young and healthy athletes doing stretching exercises in short sleeves, and they feel a little better as they battle the snow, ice and roads filled with holes large enough to swallow a Saint Bernard. They are jealous of those in Tucson, yet they are happy to see that some-where the ravaging winter is over.

Of course, Charboneau had no concept of the Indians' history. He wasn't aware of Cleveland's deplorable past, or its incredible hunger for a hero and a winner.

"All I was sure of about Cleveland was that they weren't that good a team," said Joe.

In the Minors, players know little about the Majors.

"You tend to think that everybody up there is some sort of a superman," said Joe. "When you played with a guy who had come down, you treated him with respect. You know, he had been to what we called, 'The show,' and that made him something special."

Joe spent hours talking about the Majors with his Chattanooga roommate, Dave Riveria, who was around long enough to collect a couple of monthly checks from the Texas Rangers. They discussed a time when they would play side-by-side in a big league outfield. Charboneau pleaded with Chattanooga pitcher Steve Narleski to tell him what it was like when Narleski spent the spring of 1979 with the Indians.

"I remember asking Narleski if I could hit in the show," said Joe.

"He smiled at me and said, 'Joe, you can hit anywhere, and when you are right you can hit balls out of the Grand Canyon.' That really helped my confidence."

Charboneau's Major League exposure had been limited to a few childhood excursions to Candlestick Park to watch the San Francisco Giants. He had never spoken to a Major Leaguer.

On February 16th, Joe arrived at the Indians clubhouse.

"I remember standing in front of the door. I was afraid to go in. I had never been in a Major League locker-room before. I didn't know what I thought was going to be in there, but I was really in awe. I was afraid that I might go in, and someone would say something to me, and I wouldn't know what to say back. It sounds kind of ridiculous now, but I had all these strange things running through my mind."

Joe found that Major Leaguers were indeed very human. Indians trainer Jim Warfield was the first to walk up and extend a hand to him. Pitcher Rick Waits and coaches Dave Duncan and Joe Nossek also exchanged pleasantries with him.

"It was just nice to talk with those guys," said Joe. "I felt a lot better."

Charboneau spent those early days in Tucson running up and down the stadium bleachers, catching fly balls in the outfield and taking batting practice from a pitching machine. Nothing more than a few games of catch and some running takes place early in the spring.

Nevertheless, the streamlined Charboneau did catch the attention of Gabe Paul. The 70-year-old Indians president is a fanatic about weight. When centerfielder Rick Manning reported to camp with 15 extra pounds, the story appeared in all the Cleveland papers. That was the start of Manning's year-long problems with Paul and the Indian fans. Meanwhile, Paul pointed to Charboneau as a player who obviously prepared for spring training.

Spring is far more crucial to the Indians than to most clubs. Because of their dismal past, a fast start is imperative for ticket sales. Even a winning record in exhibition games is highly encouraged, because it helps create enthusiasm in Cleveland. There is a note of desperation to all this. You can tell by all the players invited to train with the Indians.

In addition to the regulars from 1979 and the top prospects, like Charboneau and shortstop Jerry Dybzinski, there was a menagerie of bizarre characters, including Cito Gaston, Roger Moret and Hermanio Dominguez. An outfielder, Gaston had been out of baseball for much of the 1979 season. He did have a brief stint in the Inter-American League until it folded after two months. Dominguez was a tall, confused southpaw from the Mexican League, who never seemed sure of why he was in Tucson.

Moret was one of 21 pitchers brought to camp. A former star with Boston, he had pitched only 15 Major League innings since 1977. Moret had battled drug addiction, catatonic trances and an IQ which was measured to be 75. Despite 10 years in American baseball, he knew almost no English and could barely write. The Indians were told not to say anything negative or raise their voices to Moret, because they might bring back his mental problems.

"There were a lot of guys running around, but there always are in spring training," said Joe. "I don't think most of the players knew who I was, or what I did in the Minors. I met [Indians manager] Dave Garcia and he was nice, but he didn't have much to say to me. Then I read in the Tucson paper that I wasn't expected to make the team. We had not even played a game yet, and it seemed like I was in trouble. My big worry was that no one would notice me."

Charboneau's first opportunity to make an impression came on March 4th. It was just an intrasquad game. It was the first step in a marathon of spring tests. To most of the participants, it meant nothing. Dave Garcia just hoped that no one got hurt.

"Before the first intrasquad game, Cindy and I sat down and figured out that I didn't have a spot to play," said Joe. "The Indians had Mike Hargrove in leftfield, Rick Manning in center and Jorge Orta in right. You knew that all of those guys were going to play, because they were proven and getting big money. On the bench were Ron Pruitt and Dell Alston, who were on the team in 1979, and Andres Mora, who the Indians drafted from the Orioles. That made six outfielders, and they were all ahead of me in terms of experience. To those guys, the intrasquad game wasn't much, but to me it was a big deal."

Charboneau started in right field for a squad composed of the Indians rookies and reserves. He batted three times in the six-inning contest, and did the following:

• In the second inning, he lined a single to center off a Dan Spillner hanging curveball. Spillner won nine games for the Indians in 1979 and was considered the team's fifth starter for 1980.

• In the fourth inning, he drove in a run with a single to right. This time, the pitcher hanging the curveball was Larry McCall, a career 100-game winner in the Minor Leagues.

• In the sixth, he stepped into an offering by rookie Rafael Vasquez. The ball landed 400 feet from home plate, bouncing off the center field screen for a double.

That gave him 3-for-3, which was not too shabby. But he topped it the following day with a 4-for-4 performance, including a three-run 420-foot homer off the befuddled Hermanio Dominguez. Five days later, Dominguez was sent back to Mexico.

"Getting seven-straight hits was something," said Charboneau. "But I knew that the Indians would say that it was just a couple of intrasquad games and didn't mean much. Besides, Dell Alston and Ron Pruitt got hits in those games, and Andres Mora homered."

The first indication that Charboneau had indeed been an early hit came two days after the intrasquad games began. The Tribe was going to Mexico City for three exhibition games. Joe's name was among those on the list to make the trip.

"They say that it doesn't mean anything about who goes and who stays," said Joe. "But when all the regulars like Manning, Hargrove and Toby Harrah were going, while most of the young guys and long shots like Chris Bando, Cito Gaston and Rich Borchers were left behind, then you knew there was some significance."

By the end of the Indians' Mexican expedition, Charboneau would be wishing that he had remained in Tucson. Considering his first trek south of the border, Joe should have known that Mexico was not exactly the Garden of Eden.

But Joe was dazed by his incredible success in the intrasquad games. He was surprised by all the accolades and attention coming from the Cleveland media. The Indians had not yet played an exhibition game, and the *Plain Dealer* was already calling him "Super Joe," while the *Cleveland Press* settled on "Joltin' Joe." Not bad for a guy who was called only "Jo-Jo" just one year before.

So "Super-Joltin' Joe Charboneau," as a few members of the Cleveland media jokingly called him, departed with the Indians for Mexico City. As the team landed, several players discovered that they were celebrities, in the mold of Robert Redford or Pete Rose. In the Mexico City airport, they were instantly recognized and mobbed. Their pictures appeared on the front pages (not the sports pages) of most of Mexico City's 15 daily newspapers.

The heroes were Mexican natives Sid Monge, Jorge Orta and Andres Mora. Mora was greeted like another Babe Ruth, because he had pulverized Mexican League pitching during the middle 1970s before trying and flopping in baseball American-style. When Mora did play in America, the only similarity between Mexico's "Babe" Mora and the Babe who played in New York was that they both had stomachs which could hold two spare tires.

Mexico City officials gave the Indians a police escort to the Maria Isabel Hotel from the airport. Immediately, the Indians learned that there were 14 million people in Mexico City and all of them seemed to be driving at midnight. The streets were filled with Volkswagen Superbeetles and 1957 Fords and Chevys. "More clunkers here than in West Virginia," said one player.

Actually, the police escort was worthless, as there is only one Mexican traffic law. It says that no one goes anywhere with any speed. There are a few lights and stop signs, but they are ignored. The streets are anarchy. Everyone seems to be an honor graduate from the Leon Spinks driving school. Buses roll by with the doors ripped off and people hanging on to the sides. Cars crash into each other like a demolition derby, and no one stops or calls the police. Obviously, insurance is a figment of the imagination in Mexico. So are mufflers, as the city sounds like the start of the Daytona 500. A layer of pollution hangs gray and heavy over everything.

The next day, Friday, the Indians faced the Mexico City Red

Devils. As the players walked on to the field for batting practice, they immediately knew that this was not going to be an ordinary baseball game.

Behind home plate was a Mexican Military Band seated on folding chairs. They seemed to play every Latin American country's National Anthem. As they would start one song, a part of the crowd would stand up, while another portion sat down. The stadium was of Class AAA construction, and every one of its 25,000 seats was filled. Batting practice was made impossible because of the children flooding the diamond. They begged players for autographs and stole every baseball, bat and cap they came near.

Prior to the game, the Indians were presented with a four-foot "friendship trophy." It was carried off the field by the Mexican who served as Cleveland's batboy. He was fat and bald. The No. 35 on the back of his jersey matched his age.

As the action commenced, Charboneau was not in the lineup. Mora and Orta were, and they were both given standing ovations when they came to the plate. The Mexican media was obviously prepared for them. As Orta and Mora stood in the batter's box, many of the 30 photographers on the field would position themselves down the third base line only 25 feet from the hitter. A well-placed line drive would have been fatal. Autograph seekers besieged the two Indians on the field, as they ran out to their positions between innings.

The game was strange. Fly balls near the foul lines turned into battles between the Indians and fans who came on to the field trying to catch the baseballs. In the stands, fans dumped beer on each other and tossed tacos in the air whenever their Red Devils rallied. They carried portable sirens, which were sounded as the Red Devils scored. There were organized cheering sections, which banged tin plates at the command of a super fan. They didn't boo, they whistled.

When it was over, the Indians had lost, 4-0. The Tribe hit into six doubleplays and could manage only six hits off a fellow named Rene Chavez. A year earlier, Chavez had been suspended by the Mexican League for punching out an umpire on the field. Mora had two of the hits, and another went to Joe, who was sent to the plate as a pinch-hitter.

As the Indians departed from the stadium and walked toward their bus, a fan dashed by and grabbed the cap off the head of coach Dave Duncan. Gary Alexander led a group of ballplayers in a charge after the fan. They caught him, leveled him with a couple of impressive jabs and cross-over punches and then retrieved the cap.

But it was not until the next day that the Indians were fully indoctrinated into Mexican baseball. Before the first game, former Indian Ted Ford had spoken to some of his old teammates. Then a member of the Red Devils, Ford said he had never seen anything like Mexican baseball. "A new adventure every day," he said. Many of the Indians could not believe what had happened to Ford. He was 5-foot-9 and about 240 pounds, 60 pounds heavier than during his Major League days.

While March 8, 1980, will never quite live in infamy, it will be a day Joe Charboneau will never forget. It was the day he became a household name for all the wrong reasons, and the day he added yet another scar and another bizarre tale to his life.

Saturday afternoon. The Indians had changed into their uniforms at the Maria Isabel Hotel, because the dressing rooms at Mexico City Stadium resembled large closets with cracked cement floors, brick walls and a couple of leaky sinks and toilets. Rats were rumored to roam about, although none were spotted.

Charboneau and teammates Tom Brennan and Mike Stanton were standing outside the front entrance of the hotel. They were all awaiting the bus which would take them to the game. Joe was leaning against the hotel's brick wall. A grubby man, with shoulder-length black greasy hair and an unkempt beard, approached Joe. He wore a white T-shirt which was spotted with holes and black paint. His jeans were also tarnished by paint stains. He stood about 5-foot-8 and weighed about 150 pounds. In his hands were a notebook and a red Bic-pen.

"Where are you from?" he asked Joe while extending the pen and pad.

"California," replied Joe.

The man then slammed the uncapped pen into Charboneau's left side, directly below his bottom rib. Charboneau was stunned. He and the man fell to the ground.

"He's got a knife! Get the knife away from him. He's trying to get me in the eye," shouted Joe to his teammates who were standing nearby.

Brennan was the first to hop on the pile. He was followed by Stanton and *Lorain* (Ohio) *Journal* sportswriter, Hank Kozloski.

"Stanton grabbed the guy by the hair and knocked him around," said Joe. "Brennan landed a few good punches, too."

The Indians players then pinned the man to the wall. Joe was helped up, and he discovered that the pen had pierced his jersey and gone about four inches into his side. The pen, covered with blood, lay on the sidewalk. Charboneau was bleeding slightly.

"The thing that hurt me more than the stabbing was my right arm. When we hit the ground, it felt like I cracked it on the sidewalk. I thought this was it. I'm through for the rest of the spring. I figured I could forget about making the Majors."

Joe appeared more stunned than anything else by the incident. Over and over again he told people that he was all right. He kept saying, "I thought the guy just wanted an autograph, and he stabbed me with a pen. I can't believe this. I've been stabbed before, but never with a damn pen."

Charbonneau sat on the steps of the lobby waiting for an ambulance. Indians General Manager Phil Seghi was in a frenzy. He was screaming at the hotel officials to get the police and medical help. He was ignored.

Suddenly, a man in an impeccably-tailored blue suit and steel-rimmed glasses approached Joe.

"My name is Michel Fardin," he said. "I was in the newspaper stand near the lobby, and the same man who attacked you came up to me and started hitting me in the chest with his fists. Then he ran out of the lobby and went for you."

A French businessman, Fardin offered to help Joe press charges against the man. Soon a mob of people formed around Joe. The guests of the hotel all wanted to see the guy who was stuck with a pen by some lunatic.

"I felt embarrassed and ridiculous," said Joe.

After a wait of more than 50 minutes, an ambulance arrived.

"Take Joe to an American Hospital," said Phil Seghi. "I don't want him going to some Mexican joint."

Joe was driven to Mexico City's ABC Hospital. "The driver scared the hell out of me," said Joe. "He weaved in and out of traffic. I was sure we would hit something or flip over."

Arriving at the hospital, he was not impressed with the place.

"It was the dirtiest hospital I have ever seen," said Joe. "I had Sid Monge with me, and we both were shocked by how sloppy they kept the place. It was like they never dusted or washed anything. This was supposed to be the best hospital in Mexico, the one where all the American diplomats go. I remember walking by this room, and they had an operation going on. They had this guy's skull cut open, and there were no curtains around him or anything."

Joe was left in a room. Then three nurses came in and removed all his clothes, giving him a small gown that barely reached below his waist. A doctor entered and checked him. After X-rays, it was determined that there was no damage to his side or arm. He was released and given some tranquilizers and antibiotics.

About 10 minutes after Joe's departure, the police finally arrived at the hotel. They talked to the suspect. They seemed leery of the story.

"This man does not talk English," they said of Joe's attacker.

Several Cleveland players spoke up in protest, saying that they had heard the man ask Joe where he was from. Then they subsided, mumbling that they should have broken the guy in half before the cops showed up.

The man identified himself as Oscar Martinez of Chihuahua, a Mexican border province where anti-American feelings run high.

The police took Martinez to jail. When Joe returned to the hotel, he was asked to go to the police station to make the charges official. Charboneau was accompanied by Indians' Traveling Secretary Mike Seghi.

"They had me pick the guy out of a lineup," said Joe. "You know, he looked just like Charles Manson. It was really weird. He had bald spots from Brennan and Stanton pulling him by the hair."

It took more than an hour for the police to discuss the matter with Joe and Mike Seghi.

"Finally, some guy who was filling papers put on a robe and became a judge," said Seghi. "He had a trial right on the spot. Martinez said he had stabbed Joe, and that he would do it again. He said he hated all Americans, and would be back tomorrow.

"The amazing thing was that the police listened to what this guy said about wanting to get me again, and they fined him 50 pesos," said Joe. "That's $2.27, for stabbing a person. They said a pen is not a deadly weapon. They let him go after we left the station.

Soon after the incident, word of what had happened reached Gabe Paul and Bob Quinn in Tucson. Quinn was sent to tell Cindy Charboneau.

"I knew something was up when I answered my door and Bob Quinn was there," said Cindy.

"I have bad news, but don't worry," said Quinn. "There was an accident."

"Oh," gasped Cindy, on the verge of panicking.

"Joe has been stabbed, but he is okay," said Quinn. "We think some Mexican lunatic stabbed him with a hat pin."

Cindy attempted to call Joe while Quinn was still there, but the hotel line was busy. Quinn left Cindy his telephone credit card and told her to keep trying to reach Joe.

When she finally did get through, she heard the story of the guy who looked like Charles Manson, of the pen, the filthy hospital simply called ABC and the grand finale at the police station with the 50-peso fine. What she and Joe didn't know was that the Indians were ready to strike over the incident.

After Joe's stabbing, the team boarded the bus to the stadium. They refused to come out unless the security was beefed up. When they arrived at the park, they saw a legion of police. Nevertheless, many players did not want to take the field. Most felt the fans were out of control.

Indians Player Representative Wayne Garland spoke to some Mexico City baseball officials. He then addressed the Indians.

"If we don't play, they can't promise us a safe route out of here," said Garland. "They are worried what the fans would do if we don't take the field. I don't like this any more than you do, but that's the situation."

A vote via a show of hands took place. They decided to play that day's game against the Puebla Angels.

"We were scared to go out there and play, but even more scared not to," said one Indian.

So the Saturday game began two hours after the stabbing, and there were no incidents.

While Charboneau did not want his wife or anyone else to contact his mother about what had happened, the Associated Press picked up the story and sent it across the country. Soon, Mrs. Kathleen Charboneau was receiving calls from friends, telling her that her son had been stabbed with a pen, of all things, and that he was all right, and that they had heard all about it on the radio. Mrs. Charboneau then contacted Cindy, who filled her in on the details of the strange tale.

For the Indians, Sunday could not have come too soon. They had one more game to play in the city they now called, "a lunatic haven," and then they would be gone. The surprises were far from over, however.

At least Oscar Martinez and his Bib pen did not put in an appearance, but the Tribe found out that they had been hurt in another fashion.

First of all, the Mexican newspapers reported Charboneau's stabbing, but said it was prompted by Joe's refusal to sign an autograph. They made it sound like Martinez had every reason to stick Joe with the pen.

Then came the Maria Isabel's turn to stick it to the Indians. As the players checked out, they were hit with outrageous bills for extras. Wayne Garland was charged $6 for one beer. Several players were nailed with a $2 tab for each orange juice consumed.

"They got me for 900 pesos [$40] for some long distance calls I never made," said Joe. "Then there was another $7 for the use of a health spa, which was supposed to be free. They charged Rick Manning $200, and he didn't even know what it was for."

But the real shock came to manager Dave Garcia. His bill came to

$1,400. Supposedly it was from the bar, which was news to Garcia who seldom has more than an occasional beer. It seemed as though he had bought all 14 million people in Mexico City a drink.

"You just felt like giving them all your pesos and getting the hell out," said Phil Seghi.

All of the Indians except Garcia paid their ransom, and the team left for the third and final game in Mexico City. On the field, all went well, but there were problems in the front office. For making this trek, the Tribe received $15,000 up front, with another $15,000 to come at the completion of the games. The Mexicans were now withholding the final $15,000 because Garcia had not settled his alleged bar bill.

Demanding to see Garcia's bills, the Indians found that they were signed by someone named Jose Valdez, who put Garcia's room number on the checks. Garcia had never heard of Valdez, and he still has no idea of the bills' origins.

So the Indians departed without their $15,000. They had lost two of the three games. What had transpired was a classic mugging—the team had been beaten, robbed and stabbed. For this reason, they wanted to leave the "friendship trophy." Yet another argument ensued, as the Mexicans insisted that the Tribe take the trophy. At last, it was dumped in the team bus, right before it was to leave for the airport.

Jorge Orta, Sid Monge and Andres Mora were depressed over the way their countrymen had treated the Indians. The Tribe players tried to cheer them up. Charboneau said the stabbing might work out for the best. "It could get me a Bic commercial. You know, I could get stabbed with a pen, pull it out of my side and then show that it still writes."

At the airport, the customs men stopped Monge. For a time, it appeared that they wanted to place him directly in the army. They thought he was a draft-dodger. Several conversations later, that dilemma was straightened out, and the Indians departed with Monge.

"I was never so glad to get into the U.S.," said Joe. "The closest I ever want to get to Mexico again is in a Mexican restaurant."

The Indians' final present from their journey was a case of intestinal flu, which ravaged half the team during the next two weeks.

It took about a week for the Tribe to clear up their final financial settlement. When the check from Mexico City arrived, it was for $13,600—$1,400 had been deducted to pay for Garcia's bogus bar bill.

Despite all of this, Gabe Paul saw nothing odd about what had happened. "These things could have taken place anywhere," said Paul.

"The only reason Paul said that was because he wasn't on the trip," said a player.

To this day, no one is sure what happened to the "friendship trophy."

14 ★★★★★★

GARCIA

Charboneau was out for three days because of the stabbing. Further X-rays in the States showed that he had a bruised side and that the fall had loosened some bone chips in his right elbow. Nevertheless, he knew that there was no time to let any minor injuries mend.

In his second at bat after the incident, Joe lined a double to left against the Tayio Whales of Japan. He continued to impress the management.

"The strange thing about all this is that I felt like a second-class citizen," said Joe. "When the team was divided up to take batting practice, I always was sent to the Minor League field with the rest of the guys who were in trouble when it came to making the team. They kept playing me in the morning 'B' games at 10 A.M., too. They say that kind of stuff doesn't mean anything, but you know something is up when you are in one place and the regulars are in another."

Joe was growing more apprehensive by the day. Spring training just wasn't working out.

"At times, I felt like they had forgotten about me," said Charboneau. "Since the start of spring training, Dave Garcia had said about ten words to me. Like I said before, I knew that I was going to have to do something great, and do it right away, or I'd never make it.

"Well, I did hit some homers. I was hitting shots. Even getting stabbed in Mexico didn't stop me for long. But Garcia hardly noticed it."

The relationship between Joe and Garcia would take more turns than the Blue Ridge Parkway. They are generations and mentalities apart. Joe is "a punk rock ballplayer," as he would later characterize himself. Garcia is a product of the Depression and the work ethic. While Joe always felt he would be more than an average Major League player, Garcia often said that he would trade almost anything for one at bat in the big leagues.

At 60, Dave Garcia is the second oldest manager in baseball. His life is his fungo stick, his wad of chewing tobacco, his uniform and his tales of life in the bushes.

Garcia has spent 41 years in baseball and never received the attention which came to Super Joe during the first few weeks of spring training. Garcia was never a star, never a phenom and never considered a brilliant baseball man. His adjectives are "solid, dedicated and hardworking." He has little flair and little patience with attitudes he considers frivolous.

It is men like Dave Garcia which pulled America through the Depression. For him, success came late, and it was unexpected. This may be the reason he seemed suspicious of the accolades coming Charboneau's way. To fully understand Garcia's feelings about Charboneau, it is best to get to know the Indians' manager.

Garcia's attitudes, personality and almost everything else about him were shaped in those early years, growing up as one of a family of seven in a three-room rented house.

David Garcia was born September 15, 1920, in East St. Louis, Illinois. His father migrated from Piedras Blancas, Spain to East St. Louis at age 12. Benito Garcia fathered four daughters and Dave Garcia by the time he was 28. Benito was a laborer at the American Zinc Company.

"My father always had something going on the side," said Garcia. "For example, he owned a pool room. When I was eight years old, I always was around the pool room after school. I racked the balls, ran the counter and cleaned up. I also played a lot of pool. I was so small,

I'd have to stand on a Coke crate to be high enough over the table to make my shots."

At 8, Garcia was a miniature Minnesota Fats. His father knew of his son's skill with a cue stick. Benito Garcia would tell his customers they could play for free if they beat young David. If they lost, they had to pay double. "I seldom lost," recalled Garcia.

Another of Benito Garcia's hobbies was raising greyhounds. Young David helped his father with their training. Benito would keep the dogs penned up. He's send his son about 20 feet ahead of them. Then he would release the dogs and they would chase David. "I was their mechanical rabbit," Garcia said. "They must have knocked me down 100 times."

Just when Hoovervilles popped up in every town, and the Depression hung over life lower than smog in the flats, Garcia's father died. "The date was July 9, 1932," Garcia recalled. "He had had trouble with ulcers for a long time. I remember him throwing up after dinner all the time in the last year. His stomach just couldn't keep the food down."

With the death of his father, Garcia's life changed drastically.

"I never had much of a childhood to begin with," he said. "But after 1932, I was a grown man at 11 years old. Every day, I was on the corner at 5 A.M., selling newspapers. As soon as school was over, I went back to the corner and the papers, and stayed there until 6:30. On weekends, I stayed out all day."

By the time he entered high school, Garcia had found another morning job. He worked in stockyards from 6 A.M. until noon, driving cattle to their slaughter.

"Those were tough times for everyone," he said. "I never slept in a bed until I was 17. I was always in a small cot or on the floor. I made $10 a week selling papers. My mother worked in a shirt factory, and I made more money than she did.

"She was a marvelous woman. We had only two bedrooms and a kitchen, an outdoor toilet, a wood stove and little money. But we made it. I'm ashamed to admit this, but we had help from what would now be called the welfare department. They gave us $32 a month, and that always made sure we'd have enough for the rent."

Garcia never played high school sports. He spent most of his free time kicking a soccer ball or tossing a baseball in the streets or on the sandlots.

"I was a bad kid when it came to school," he said. "If my kids did some of the things I did, I'd break their legs. For example, I never took a book home from school. For book reports, I'd make up a story line, an author and all the rest right before class.

"I knew the English teacher never read all the books that had been written, and I never got caught. A book I did read was *Last of the Mohicans,* by James Fenimore Cooper. For six straight years, I turned in a book report on it. I did like history. I used to take my history book home over the summer and read it. I liked the stories.

"Generally, I was a tough little kid," added Garcia. "After selling my papers, I'd sneak into the movies and stay there all night. But I gave every dime I made as a kid to my mother. Then she'd give me a little back."

Garcia graduated from high school in 1937. For two years, he worked as a beef lugger. "I'd carry about 250,000 pounds of meat around a day," he said. "I know that sounds amazing, but each load was between 100 and 300 pounds."

In 1938, Garcia went to a St. Louis Browns tryout camp and was offered a contract. His baseball career came to an abrupt end when a baseball hit his skull in spring training.

"I couldn't get my pro career going," he said. "After getting beaned, I was released. The next year, I got another chance at pro ball. This time, I went to Lake Charles, Louisiana and ripped the cartilage in my knee after four games."

Garcia spent the 1940 season at home. He played softball and semi-pro baseball for a team called the Burke Undertakers. In 1941, his friendship with former Yankee and East St. Louis native Hank Bauer got him a tryout with a Class D team in East Grand Forks, Minnesota. A week later, he was traded for a guy named Lefty Foell to Eau Claire, Wisconsin.

"I had knee problems again in 1941," he said. "In 1942, I was healthy and batted .320 for Eau Claire with 18 homers and 107 runs batted in. Then I got drafted."

Garcia was a member of the Army Air Corps. He served as a supply officer overseas, about 100 miles behind the front lines. In 1946, he was out of the army and back in pro baseball. He has never left the game since.

Baseball front offices love men like Garcia. When they need a manager in Oshkosh, a coach in Fresno or a scout in Latin America, he is there to fill the role. It took Garcia until 1970 to reach the Majors, and that was as a member of the San Diego Padres coaching staff.

His first Major League manager's job came with the California Angels in 1977, when he took over for Norm Sherry at mid-season. He was fired on May 31, 1978. His team was 1½ games out of first place. He took the axing like a true baseball organization man.

Garcia is a manager again. It is hard to imagine him as anything else.

"You know, I'm not bitter or anything like that about the things that have happened to me," he said. "I remember in 1957, I was driving a taxi in the off-season to pick up some extra money.

"I had this priest in my cab. I was talking to him, telling him about my early life. He looked at me and said, 'Son, the books will balance.'

"From that day, good things just keep happening to me. I've been lucky. Yes, the books have balanced."

Two weeks into the spring, Joe's concern increased, when Garcia proclaimed Andres Mora the team's No. 4 outfielder, behind starters Jorge Orta, Mike Hargrove and Rick Manning.

"I couldn't see where Mora was having a better spring than me," said Joe. "I just had this feeling that they didn't want me to make the team. I wasn't in their plans. The only guy from the front office who talked to me was Bob Quinn."

In a March 19th game in Mesa, Arizona vs. the Cubs, Charboneau homered over the centerfield fence sign 410 feet from home plate. While the pitcher was a left-hander named George Riley, who will never be mistaken for Steve Carlton, the gargantuan smash was awesome, considering it came off a changeup. He was 11-for-23 with two homers and 8 RBIs, but only 3-for-9 in "A" games.

"What really began to get to me was that they wouldn't put my stats in intrasquad and 'B' games into my spring totals," said Joe. "I know this wasn't the case, but I was at the point where I thought they made that rule just to keep me from looking good.

"The pressure was tremendous. Before I hit the homer against the Cubs, I could barely swing the bat my first two times up because my stomach was so tight. Now and then, I was throwing up before games because I was so nervous. I would go home at night, and Cindy and I would go over the roster, trying to figure out how I could make the final 25. It was nerve-racking."

Two days after his "Mesa Mash," Joe had three hits in a game, including a pair of doubles. He was 15-for-32 over all, when he received a boost from Cliff Johnson. During the winter, Johnson broke and almost severed the middle finger of his right hand while lifting a barrel of oats off of a truck. He was recovering slowly, and then he did not show up for the first week of spring training. He was fined $1,000. However, Johnson had not played much all spring due to his injury, and it now became apparent that he would not be ready for opening day.

For the first time, Garcia publicly praised Joe.

"Charboneau is everything they said he was," said Garcia. "The boy can hit. It doesn't matter who is on the mound. He goes up there with confidence, and he has a good chance of making our club."

The date of Garcia's statement was March 21, 1980. Nevertheless, Joe still worried.

"Garcia never said anything to me directly," said Joe. "I later found out that it is just his way, not to talk to rookies, but at the time, our lack of communication bugged me. When Cindy and I worked on our rosters, we figured out that either Dave Rosello, Dell Alston or I could be cut. Rosello and Alston were with the team in 1979, so I didn't think I had anything sewed up."

Two weeks before the end of spring training, Joe heard from his old agent that he was being sent to the Indians Class AAA Tacoma club. Gary Alexander was to be the DH, he was told. Joe then made arrangements for an apartment in that Northwest city.

"At this point I was really confused," said Joe. "My agent was

telling me I was going to be farmed out. Some other guys were saying
that I had made the team. Garcia and the front office weren't saying
anything. It got to the point that I didn't even want to hear about it."

With ten days left, Joe's break came, as Indians first baseman
Andre Thornton went down with a knee injury. He needed surgery.
Plans were made to move Mike Hargrove in from left field to first
base, and to try Charboneau and Mora in left. Joe hit a pair of homers
down the stretch to win the job.

"The amazing part about all this is that I did not find out I had
made the team until three days before the start of the season. I was
lying on the trainer's table and Garcia walked in and told me that I
would be starting in left field for the opener against the Angels.

"Baseball is really strange. I believe that before the spring starts the
front office has the twenty-five guys in mind that they think should
make the team. It takes something sensational to change their minds.
During the middle of the spring, I would have cut off my arm to be the
twenty-fifth. I spent the spring worrying that I would hear that they
had cleaned out my locker. That is the sign that you've been cut. They
were talking about me being the fifth outfielder. Then all of a sudden I
was a starter and batting cleanup."

Before the opener, Garcia dropped Charboneau out of the fourth
spot in the order to No. 7, to relieve some of the pressure on the
rookie. At this point, Joe didn't care where he batted. He was happy
just to be on the club.

15 ⭐⭐⭐⭐⭐⭐

OPENING, WEST COAST

ANAHEIM, CALIFORNIA, April 11 — Indians rookie Joe Charboneau today made his Major League debut an auspicious one by hitting a home run in just his second Major League at-bat.

OPENING DAY 1980

There are 37,085 fans in the stands at Anaheim Stadium to see the defending American League West champion California Angels open their season against the Cleveland Indians. It is the first time within anyone's memory that the Indians are beginning on the West Coast. Batting seventh in Manager Dave Garcia's lineup is the lone rookie starting in this game, Joe Charboneau. What a day in the life of the kid from Santa Clara, who was cut by two Little League coaches, who sold frogs for 25¢ each to pay for his first baseball spikes and whose career appeared finished when he quit the game just three years ago.

The Santa Ana winds are blowing hard on this sunny California day, and among those sitting in the stands are the three people who mean the most to Joe Charboneau . . . his mother, Kathleen, his wife, Cindy, and his son, Tyson, who is now seven months old. Joe has given out 25 passes for his debut. There are two sets of aunts, numerous cousins, other relatives and friends.

Super Joe is nervous. It's not every day a kid makes the jump from Chattanooga of the Class AA Southern League to the big time.

"I couldn't wait for that first Major League base hit," he said. "I would have taken anything . . . a broken bat hit, something off the handle, a dribbler, anything. I had visions of going a week without a hit."

With two out in the second inning, Joe steps into a Major League batting box for the first time. The Angels pitcher is a right-hander, Dave Frost. Just six months ago, Frost was hurling for the Angels in the American League playoffs. Frost works the count to two strikes. On the next pitch, the rookie hits a ground ball to third baseman Carney Lansford. Lansford, fielding it cleanly, easily throws Charboneau out. It's not the first time Carney Lansford has ever gunned down Super Joe. The two were opponents during their high school days in Northern California.

Three innings later, the Angels are sitting on a 5-0 lead when Joe steps up to the plate for the second time. There is one out, no one on base, and the Indians have managed to get just one hit off Frost.

Frost, a 16-game winner in 1979, runs the count to 2-and-1, then comes in with a low-away fastball. Super Joe, taking a nice fluid swing, launches the ball toward the fence in right-centerfield. It looks like a fading Tom Watson 4-iron shot. The ball carries easily over the fence, more than 400 feet away. The kid has homered in his second Major League at bat. "Normally," said Joe. "I don't smile on home runs. This time I did, though."

Indians relief pitcher Sid Monge dashed over to retrieve the baseball, presenting it to the rookie in the late innings of the 10-2 loss. In addition to hitting his first big league home run on this day, Joe registered his first big league strikeout, fanning in the ninth inning off Angels reliever Mark Clear.

The remaining two games in Anaheim would not dazzle Rookie of the Year voters. Following the home run, Charboneau went 0-for-8, ending the California trip with a single in the eighth inning of the third game, off Angels reliever John Montague.

Adding insult to an already sinking situation, Super Joe moved into the leftfield corner to pick up a double, hit in the third game, and was spat upon by a girl and two men sitting in seats near the corner. "That," he says, "is when I knew I had arrived in the big leagues."

ARLINGTON, TEXAS, April 15 — The first slump. The kid who hit a home run in his second Major League at bat is now 2-for-14 on the season.

The Indians have won only one of their first five games and have gone 16 consecutive innings without scoring a run. Joe is pressing. He maintains that he is not worried. "Every year I'm a slow starter," he says. "Last year I went 2-for-24. One of the big differences is that in the Minor Leagues, there was the security of knowing that when you went into a slump, you were still in there. Here there is no security. I may be putting too much pressure on myself. At first I couldn't believe I was in the big show. In the back of my mind I keep thinking Andy Thornton will be coming back."

Everyone offers advice to Super Joe. Skipper Dave Garcia says, "If I were Charboneau, I would never look at the newspapers. He shouldn't even think about who is pitching. He should just go up there and swing the bat like he did in spring training. That boy should have no worries. In the spring, he didn't care who was pitching. He hit them all."

Indians Captain Duane Kuiper notes, "All Joe needs is a couple of base hits and he'll be fine. The thing is, a rookie is always under more pressure when he starts slow. If a veteran starts slow, everyone has patience. I think Joe is a natural hitter," continued Kuiper. "He'll hit for a high average, and he'll hit 25 home runs, too. You know, Joe hit a homer in his second at bat in the Majors, and maybe he thought that he was going to do that all the time. Well, it's not that easy."

Super Joe closes out the Indians' first road trip of the season by hitting a single in two official trips, in the final game at Arlington. The Indians are 1–5 on the season. The pitching staff's ERA is 7.09, and the phenom comes home batting .200 with one home run, two RBIs and five strikeouts in his first half-dozen games.

16 ★★★★★★★

CLEVELAND OPENING

CLEVELAND, OHIO, April 19 — Rookie Joe Charboneau raps a home run, a double, a single and knocks in two runs to lead the Indians to an 8–1 victory over the Toronto Blue Jays.

Charboneau is big on openings.

The 1980 home opener in Cleveland was played on the third Saturday in April. The day was clear; the temperature was 73 degrees. Major League baseball's largest opening day crowd, 61,753 was in the 48-year-old Cleveland Stadium.

Huge gatherings in the 76,000-seat stadium are nothing new. The once-glorious franchise drew an American League record 2,620,627 fans during the 1948 World Championship season. A Major League record 84,587 witnessed a doubleheader against the New York Yankees in 1954, and a Major League record for a night game was set in 1948 when the Indians hosted Chicago before 78,382 fans.

In 1973, an opening day crowd set a Major League record when 74,420 poured through the turnstiles to see the Indians play the Detroit Tigers. The franchise, which hasn't had a contending team in two decades, has fallen on hard times, however. Only twice in the past 20 years has it drawn more than 1 million fans for a season. Baseball fans in

Cleveland are hungry for a winner, hungry for a personality to rally behind.

The size of the Stadium stunned Joe. The largest crowd he had ever played before up to the 1980 season was 10,000 at a Southern League All-Star game in Nashville, during the 1979 season. "I liked the Stadium the first time I saw it," said Joe. "I had a good feeling about playing in it."

This home opener turned out to be the most memorable since Frank Robinson, Major League baseball's first black manager, homered in his first at bat as player-manager in 1975.

But this day belonged to Joe Charboneau, an athlete who had never seen Cleveland or its Grand Canyon of a Stadium until one day before he was to play there. This was a headline day for Charboneau, the man they call Super Joe. It was a day he would always cherish, a day that would live on in the form of a wall plaque, containing the newspaper account of the contest, which hangs in his living room. Most of all, it was a day when Joe Charboneau discovered what it meant to be a Major Leaguer and a star. It was a day Clevelanders found a reason to stand up and cheer and to feel good about themselves and their baseball team.

You are more likely to find snow than sun in April in Cleveland, but the sun gleamed on this day. And the fans responded. They came from the suburbs, the city, the projects and the far East-Side mansions. They came to take off their shirts and drink beer, while absorbing the warmth in the bleachers. They came to forget about the snow, the potholes, inflation and Iran. They came hungry for a new hero. Yes, this was to be a great day, a super day. It was also to be the day Cito Gaston had one last hurrah.

Because his bats remained in Tucson while the team began the season, Joe had been "swinging anything I could get my hands on." Three weeks before opening day, Cito Gaston was cut by the Indians. The amiable and aging outfielder saw his distinguished career end with not even a whimper, but with a quick and quiet exit. He left camp like a shadow, and few noticed his absence. All that remained were his bats. He knew he would never need them again. It was over for him, but his bats traveled with the rest of the Indians' lumber.

On opening day in Cleveland, a slumping Joe Charboneau held a bat, with "Cito Gaston" branded on its barrel, in his hands. It felt good and right, like an extension of his blacksmith's arms.

In his first at bat before the Cleveland crowd, Charboneau was greeted with a giant cheer and several signs which read WE LOVE YOU, SUPER JOE. Not bad for a guy who had yet to play a game before these people. Five pitches later, Joe Charboneau was on first base with a walk.

In the fifth inning, Charboneau lashed a double and then scored a run, which put the Indians ahead, 2-1. But it was the sixth inning which became the first chapter of the Super Joe legend in Cleveland.

On the mound for Toronto was Tom Buskey, a former football player at the University of North Carolina and a former Indian. Before the end of 1980, Tom Buskey would also be a former Major League pitcher. Charboneau took a Buskey fastball over the centerfield fence. The fans were on their feet. It was an orgy of joy and thanks, that the player they so wanted to do well had succeeded. The old Stadium rocked until it seemed like it would give way. Super Joe had touched all four bases and returned to the dugout, and the place was still shaking. The 61,753 fans wanted Joe.

"Go on, take a bow," urged teammates Rick Manning and Toby Harrah. Out of the dugout, to the chants of "Super Joe, Super Joe," stepped the man himself. Off came his cap and up went the volume.

When the game was over, Charboneau found more writers around his locker than he thought ever existed. He talked of his homer and of his single and double. He talked about what a great place Cleveland was and said he didn't realize that he was just a triple away from hitting for the cycle. A 3-for-3 performance raised his batting average from .200 to .304.

"Before the start of the year, I told Cindy that if I was in the lineup I'd win Rookie of the Year for her," said Joe to some friends. "I never wanted to be an average ballplayer. I always wanted to be a star."

The scribes immediately began comparing Super Joe to the charismatic Rocky Colavito. Colavito patrolled rightfield for the Indians in the late 1950s. He was traded by General Manager Frank Lane for Harvey Kuenn after the 1959 season, in which Rocky ripped 42 homers and knocked in 111 runs at age 26. The last time the Indians were in contention was 1959, and fans still point and say that the day baseball died in Cleveland was when Rocky Colavito was traded. Even Rocky's return to Cleveland in 1965 could not revive the situation.

MILWAUKEE, WISCONSIN, April 23 — A three-run home run by rookie Joe Charboneau propels the Indians to a 7–3 victory over the Milwaukee Brewers.

The Indians had lost three in a row. Their record was now 2–8, and they were in need of a shot, any sort of shot. The shot came from Super Joe's bat. It was a three-run home run in the fourth inning off Brewers pitcher Moose Haas, and it insured free-agent prospect Dan Spillner of his first win.

Writers covering the Indians on this night were in for quite a surprise upon entering the clubhouse following the game. The hero of the night lay on the floor, pinned by several of his teammates. He was being covered with spaghetti, shaving cream and the remnants of a tossed salad. The kid was being initiated.

"That's when I felt I was really part of the team," said Joe. "The hot spaghetti burned my back, but I didn't mind one bit. I thought of it as a kind of Italian baptism."

The initiation ceremonies ended, and the players began stripping to take their showers. The floor was strewn with pants, shirts, socks and jock straps. But Joe refused to shower. With spaghetti, shaving cream and tossed salad still on his back, he slipped into his slacks. "I want to remember this," he said. His intentions were to fly home with the spaghetti and all covering the upper part of his bare body. Approaching a mirror in the clubhouse, in order to brush a couple of meat balls and some spaghetti sauce from his head, he ran into Skipper Garcia.

Garcia, somewhat puzzled at what he was seeing, said, "What are you doing, kid?"

"Well," said Joe. "I figured I would go home like this."

Suddenly, Indians playful utility player Ron Pruitt yelled, "Okay, let's get about ten or twelve guys and throw him in the shower." It did not take Charboneau's teammates long to gain respect for his strength, but the kid was showered and flew home without his spaghetti.

"The guys had been treating me great all along," said Joe, who loves this side of baseball. "But this really made me feel good."

CLEVELAND, OHIO, April 27 — Super Joe Charboneau, now hitting .354 with three home runs and eight RBIs, sat out his first game of the season with the flu.

It took Joe only two games to shake the flu. However, it took him longer to shake the after-effects. Upon returning to the lineup, Joe not only stopped hitting, he began striking out with alarming regularity. Dave Steib fanned him three straight times in Toronto. The following day, coming to the plate with the bases loaded twice, and once with two on, he left 10 men stranded.

In Cleveland, Joe found that he needed a friend and advisor. His finances were a disaster when he asked Dan Donnelly, a local heating and cooling contractor, to officially represent him and help him watch over his money. Up to this point, Joe had not been able to deal with bills as well as fastballs.

"My finances were a mess," he admitted. "I was making more money than I had ever made, and I just couldn't handle it."

Charboneau was spending his $21,000 salary as though it was $210,000. A VISA charge card, along with its $1,000 limit, was taken away.

"I had become a real sucker," admitted Joe. "I'd take $400 on the road and halfway through the trip look in my wallet and wonder where the money went."

The rookie picked up a $300 bar check in Chicago. He was buying things on impulse. He was living from paycheck to paycheck. "I needed someone to help me."

The someone turned out to be Donnelly, a 34-year-old reformed alcoholic, who had begun a heating and cooling business with his last $1,000 in 1974. At the time, he had one employee and one truck. Dan now owns an $850,000 business with fourteen employees and a dozen trucks.

"Joe was something of a sap when it came to green flies hanging on," said Donnelly, who had never represented an athlete before.

The two met in spring training at Tucson. They quickly became friends. "Why don't you be my agent?" asked Joe. Donnelly said he'd let him know.

"I didn't know anything about representing ballplayers," said Donnelly. "All I knew about were furnaces and air-conditioners."

Finally, Donnelly agreed to take over Charboneau's finances. "I didn't know what I was getting into," said Donnelly. "But Joe is an unusual individual, and I couldn't help liking him. It's hard to turn him down if he needs help with anything.

"I don't depend on this for a living," said Donnelly. "Actually, I am probably losing money by handling him. It's funny, to his fans he's Super Joe. To those of us close to him, though, he's nothing but a big baby."

At the time Donnelly agreed to handle Super Joe's finances, the rookie was being besieged with offers from big-time agents. One offered a $20,000 interest-free loan. Another promised to set him up with hookers wherever the Indians played.

Yet another said he would give Donnelly $1,000 if Joe would sign with a certain firm. At one time or another, twenty different agents were dangling baubles in front of Joe.

"One of the reasons I wanted Dan was his own background," said Joe. "He made it as a successful businessman on his own. I liked that. I trusted him, whereas I didn't trust all those other guys who were offering me the sky."

Donnelly had already aided Super Joe immensely, prior to their agreement. Dan had arranged for Joe and Cindy to live at the Sheraton Rocky River Hotel. Hotel Manager Gerry Thomas was a friend of Donnelly's. He let the Charboneaus reside there rent-free.

"I was getting a good feeling for the city of Cleveland from the way people treated us at the hotel," said Joe. "They were very nice, but we were glad when Dan got us into an apartment."

"At the time," said Donnelly, "All they owned were some pots, pans, blankets and a few clothes. And they kept most of their things in the back of a pickup truck. They didn't even have a refrigerator to keep the baby's formula in."

Soon thereafter, Donnelly placed the Charboneaus in a condominium he owned on the Lake Erie Gold Coast. He also dressed Joe up. "All the guy had was a basic wardrobe of Levis and T-shirts."

Super Joe did have one suit. He had bought it at a Salvation Army store in Santa Clara for $20. The slacks were too small, the coat too big. He wore that suit, along with a 99¢ tie that had a shark on it, to the team's welcome-home luncheon.

Dan Donnelly took his new client to a men's clothes shop and helped him pick out three suits that cost considerably more than $20 apiece.

"The guy was really messed up when I took over for him," said Donnelly. "He was getting a lot of requests to make personal appearances and couldn't say no to any of them. He was even trying to do two at the same time, without realizing it."

The demand for Joe was indeed growing out of hand. He was earning $500 to sign autographs at a car dealership for two hours. He was sought after for cocktail parties, bar mitzvahs and even Ohio Senator John Glenn, the former astronaut, wanted Charboneau to endorse him.

"We turned down a lot of requests," said Donnelly. "Many of them were not in good taste, and they would be taking too much of his time."

Joe's popularity, nonetheless, was soaring. A fan club, with 350 members, had been formed. It was the largest in the history of the franchise. Dan Donnelly was finding his new client to be as time-consuming as the heating and cooling business.

Dan Donnelly's popularity grew as well. He started Lake Sports Management when he became Joe's agent. Since then, Dan has become the agent for a number of sports personalities. From the Indians, he represents pitcher Mike Stanton, an artist in his spare time. Von Hayes, a young, rising star in the Indian organization, and Scott Ullger of the Minnesota Twins farm system. He also represents Andy Gissinger of Syracuse University, a possible high-round draft choice, Tom Moriarty of the Pittsburgh Steelers, and Pat Moriarty, a run-

ning back with the 1979 Browns, who made the team as a free
agent. Finally, he has signed contracts with Myra van Hoose, the 1980
Rookie of the Year on the Ladies Professional Golf Association tour,
and Scott De Candia, the 1980 National Long Drive Champion.

BAR SCENE

OAKLAND, CALIFORNIA, May 5 — Super Joe Charboneau
went 0-for-4, fanning two more times. In his last 23 trips to the plate,
he has recorded three hits, struck out 10 times and driven in just one
run. His batting average has dropped from .354 to .286 in seven
games.

For the first time, Manager Dave Garcia benched his rookie.

"Going into a slump like that and striking out like I was striking out was nothing new," said Joe. "Several years before in Visalia, I struck out seven times in eight at bats. Then, Eddie Bockman visited me. I hit four home runs and drove in ten during the next four days."

This was not Visalia, however, and Joe was beginning to doubt whether or not he could handle Major League pitching.

"Pitchers were throwing curveballs, and I'd miss. Then I'd be looking for the curveball and they'd throw a fastball. I was getting confused. I was having trouble distinguishing between balls and strikes. My frame of mind was bad. I felt like staying home or going back to my mother's house."

Garcia inserted Charboneau back into the lineup the following day at

Oakland, May 7th. He went 0-for-3, fanning twice. Joe was now batting
.274.

*SEATTLE, WASHINGTON, May 8 — Indians Manager Dave
Garcia, hearing that Super Joe Charboneau is becoming a regular
part of the bar scene, calls the rookie down for a lecture.*

The .274 batting average did not sit well with Super Joe Charboneau.
Nor did the 11 strikeouts in his seven previous games. Nor did the fact
that he had now gone more than two weeks without a home run.

May 8th was an off-day, and the Indians flew that morning from
Oakland to Seattle, where they stayed at the Seattle Hilton Hotel. At
about 1 P.M. that afternoon, Joe stopped in the cocktail lounge of the
hotel and had two beers with a couple of the coaches. Then he left to
spend the rest of the afternoon with his sister Carol.

Charboneau was not present much later that day, when a member of
the Seattle Hilton's security force routed Skipper Garcia from bed to tell
him that several of his ballplayers were being obnoxious in the hotel bar.
Garcia arrived to find a couple of writers, a few broadcasters and Rick
Manning. There was no rowdiness, so Garcia once again retired.

However, on the following day, Garcia was informed that Charboneau had been in the bar at 11 A.M. to drown his sorrows. Before that
night's game against the Seattle Mariners, the manager told the rookie
that he better straighten out or he would lose out to the bottle. The kid
was disturbed.

"Garcia never asked about what I did that day," said Joe. "All of his
information was on hearsay. He talked to me about my night life. I
never argue with a manager, but my night life is my own business. And
really, there is nothing unusual about my night life. He thought I was
drinking real heavy, but I wasn't.

"I enjoy a few beers, but I never go into a bar alone," continued Joe. "I
get my twelve hours of sleep a night. I might not go to bed until three in
the morning, but I do it on purpose. I like to sleep until three in the
afternoon, get up, watch soap operas and then go right to the ball park."

This was not the first time Garcia had jumped on the rookie. He had seen the kid carrying a sixpack of beer to his room a week before in Toronto. He chewed him out for that. Super Joe had been extremely upset over this. So much so that Coach Duncan had telephoned his agent, Dan Donnelly, to calm Joe down.

"I thought I was ninety percent calmer than I used to be," said Joe. "Dave is a funny guy. I never questioned his lifestyle, but now he was questioning mine. And after not saying a thing to me during the spring, he said I wasn't getting enough sleep on the road. Actually, I wasn't getting enough sleep at home. Tyson was up three times a night, and because we were in a hotel, and all in one room, I'd be getting up with him."

The problem between these two personalities was a simple one. A man of 60 does not think on the same level as a youngster of 24. The generation gap had taken over.

Dave Garcia had been in organized baseball for more than 40 years as a player, coach, Minor League manager and now big league manager. He breathed baseball. He showed up at the ball park at noon for night games, making sure every need was taken care of for each player. His ambition as manager was to get the most out of his ballplayers as often as he could. The fear of losing his job never bothered him.

"I know some day I will get fired," he said. "It's just a matter of time. And when I do, what I want most is to be able to go back to coaching third base for someone. I love to coach third base."

In Super Joe Charboneau, Dave Garcia saw a potentially fine ballplayer whose career was being threatened by things like overexposure to booze and the media. Garcia told one writer, "I know you guys have a job to do, but I think all the nicknames and everything else attached to this kid will hurt him in the long run."

Joe never felt comfortable around Garcia. He said, in fact, "I don't think Dave really wanted me to make the team. At times, I just think he hated my guts. Why he didn't like me, I don't know. Maybe it was that I was getting too much publicity."

The pre-game admonition may or may not have had any sort of effect. For the moment, however, it seemed to. For the first time in more than two weeks, Charboneau had two hits in a single game. He doubled, then smashed his fourth home run of the season, a two-run blow off Seattle lefty Floyd Bannister. More problems were to follow, though.

CLEVELAND, OHIO, May 15 — Mike Hargrove's 23-game hitting streak is halted, and Super Joe Charboneau once again is benched. This time for four games against the Boston Red Sox.

Joe was on a 3-for-14 non-streak. So he, along with designated hitter Cliff Johnson, were both banished from the lineup. Johnson, batting .214 with one home run and seven RBIs at the time, was sat down for not running out a ground ball the previous night. Super Joe was benched for not hitting. He was now hitting .275 with four home runs and 14 RBIs.

Charboneau was puzzled. It had been a long time since he had been sitting so much. The last time this had happened was in Peninsula, when he quit.

"Maybe I'd be better off going back to Tacoma," he said to Dan Donnelly, his agent. To Cindy, Joe said, "I am no longer enjoying the game like I used to. Maybe I should go back where I can have some fun."

Super Joe finally sat down and talked with teammate Toby Harrah, a 10-year veteran to whom many young Indians go for advice. Harrah told him to wait it out, as he was sure to receive another chance.

Looking back at the situation, Donnelly said, "At the time, he was really down, really depressed. He wanted to play all the time. He had played through slumps before, and he couldn't understand why he wasn't permitted to play through this one."

Following the May 16th game against the Red Sox in Cleveland, a game in which Charboneau didn't play, Joe asked Donnelly to take Cindy home. Joe wanted to go off by himself.

Donnelly refused.

"To be honest, I was afraid Joe would just go to a bar and drink his troubles away," said Donnelly. "Actually, Joe did not go out drinking that night. He went to work on his weights. Joe worries about his slumps. He has a lot of confidence, but in the back of his mind he fears failure. On one side, he is cocky, but on the other he needs people around him to keep up his confidence."

Joe and Donnelly would spend hours talking about the season and what was happening both on the field and off. As the year wore on, Donnelly and Charboneau were inseparable. On an average day, Joe would telephone Donnelly three or four times.

"Dan is my best friend in Cleveland," said Joe. "He understands me and Cindy very well. We go over to his house and have dinner with him and Elizabeth, his wife. When I'm on the road, they watch over Cindy and Tyson and sometimes take them over to their house. They keep Cindy from getting lonely."

"Joe is a tough critic of himself," said Donnelly. "He expects perfection. When he doesn't get a hit, he will get down. Then I'll try to cheer him up, and tell him he hit the ball hard even if he didn't get a hit. The thing that makes him feel better than anything else is kids. He'll have a bad day and then he'll go out for an appearance. He'll see those kids, and he'll light up. They make him feel good, and he relates well to them.

"It is amazing," continued Donnelly. "We will be driving around and he'll see a Little League game and tell me to stop. Then he'll go out and see the kids. He says it picks him up. He remembers when he was a kid and he would think about how it would have been if a big league player had stopped at his Little League game. That's why he does things like that."

Cindy is well aware of the way Joe is prone to depression during rough times. She knows the magic children work upon him.

"After a bad day, I will try to talk to him about it," said Cindy. "But sometimes it doesn't do any good. That's when I bring out Tyson. Tyson always makes him feel good again. I know that Joe sometimes comes off as being cocky, but he is a dedicated husband and father. He worries about Tyson and me all the time. He wants to do well, not just for himself, but for us. He is so determined, and that's why he takes slumps hard."

Cindy and Dan Donnelly were not the only people in Joe's corner during the year. The fans stayed behind him. At times, this unmitigated support confused Joe, while buoying him all the same.

"I didn't ask for all this publicity. I just wanted to be a normal ballplayer," said Joe, forgetting his earlier dreams. "In fact, I was getting upset that nothing bad was being written about me. I deserved it. I had been playing lousy. Not even any of my fan mail was bad. Not a single piece. Oh, I did get a bad letter from a fag in Chicago once, but even he didn't mean any harm. It was amazing how everyone stuck with me."

18 ★★★★★

STRIKE

BOSTON, MASSACHUSETTS, May 23 — Major League base-
ball's first strike was averted today when the owners and the Players
Association agreed to a new contract.

The threat of a strike had hung over the more than 600 Major League
ballplayers from the time they walked out of spring training, ten days
before opening day. They had set May 23rd as the deadline for reaching
a new basic agreement with the baseball owners.

Young ballplayers, such as Joe Charboneau and Jerry Dybzinski,
were painfully aware that a strike at this point could be disastrous to
their careers.

"It crossed my mind a lot," said Joe, who was making the Major
League minimum of $21,000 at the time. "Here I was, finally on a Major
League roster, and then we were going to strike. It seemed like some
more of the old Charboneau rotten luck."

The approaching deadline led to widespread speculation.

"I figured we were going out," said Joe. "I was all set to work for Dan
Donnelly."

Other Indians were also ready to return home. Catcher Gary Alexander, earning $82,500 a year, was prepared to go to Los Angeles and

take a job as a stage hand for NBC-TV, where he would make $12.50 an hour. "And if I am actually forced to do that," said Alexander, who is not strong on economics, "I just might say to hell with baseball."

In the early morning hours of May 23rd, the strike threat ended. The owners and players had reached a new basic agreement. Among the new terms was a clause that raised the minimum salary from $21,000 to $30,000. Super Joe and Dybzinski, the Indians rookie duo, took a lot of good-natured static from their teammates prior to that night's game against the Red Sox in Boston's Fenway Park.

"Look at you two guys," said Duane Kuiper, "A $9,000 raise right in the middle of the season. You've got us old veterans to thank for that."

Indians Traveling Secretary Mike Seghi approached Super Joe before the game with an appearance request that was worth $400. "What do I need that for. I just got a $9,000 raise," quipped Joe.

BOSTON, MASSACHUSETTS, May 24 — Rookie Joe Charboneau raps out two hits, including a home run, and drives in three runs while leading the Indians to a 7–2 victory over Boston.

It didn't take Joe long to celebrate his raise. The home run off Red Sox veteran Jack Billingham was his sixth of the season, pushing his RBI total to 21. His batting average was .297. There was not a rookie in the American League carrying better marks to this point in the season.

Three days later, in Baltimore, Joe unloaded off 1980 Cy Young Award-winner Steve Stone in Cleveland's come-from-behind 7–6 victory. The following night, this time against three-time Cy Young Award-winner Jim Palmer, the rookie belted number eight in a 10–6 victory.

Orioles Coach Frank Robinson was impressed.

"His power reminds me of myself a few years ago," said Robby, the only player ever to win the MVP Award in both the American and National Leagues.

Charboneau's home run off Palmer gave him a special thrill. "I like to hit good pitchers," said Joe. "I feel they make me concentrate more."

Several of the rookie's 23 home runs were off the game's quality pitchers. Besides Palmer and Stone, Charboneau belted two off 1979 Cy

Young Award-winner Mike Flanagan and one off the Royals' Paul Splittorff.

It wasn't enough to lead the club in home runs and rank second in RBIs, however. Followers of the team still could not understand why Joe remained in the seventh spot of the batting order and why he was benched against right-handed pitchers.

Skipper Garcia, explaining why he kept his rookie near the bottom of the lineup, said, "I'm not saying that down the line he won't bat fourth, but right now I'm going to keep him lower in the lineup. By having him there, the pressure isn't as great, and I think this means something when you're dealing with a young ballplayer."

"Two years ago at Vasalia, I batted fifth and knocked in 118 runs for 130 games," said Joe, exuding diplomacy. "There are a lot of RBIs down there. Besides, I love batting behind Toby Harrah. He's helped me a lot. He tells me what to look for when I get up there. And when he's on base, he's so smart. He knows how to run, how to steal. I don't mind batting down there at all."

The emergence of Miguel Dilone and the presence of designated hitter Cliff Johnson presented lineup problems for Garcia, whose club was struggling to stay at the .500 mark. Dilone, a leftfielder picked up from the Chicago Cubs for $35,000, was hitting an astounding .340 and was en route to setting a club record for stolen bases. And Johnson, a 32-year-old veteran who was outstanding in the second half of 1979 after the Indians acquired him from the Yankees, was expected to break out of a slump which had him batting around the .200 mark.

"I feel that if I go more than two games in a row without a hit I will be on the bench," said Joe in early June.

Charboneau's batting average was beginning to drop as Garcia sat him down against certain pitchers. By mid-June, he was at .264, the lowest his average would fall all season.

Following a three-run homer that led the Indians to an 8–5 victory over Kansas City on June 11th, Garcia was asked why Charboneau, despite leading the club with nine home runs and ranking second with 28 RBIs, was held back against certain pitchers.

"Joe hits lefties well," said Garcia. "Some righties give him trouble. Look, Rick Manning and Jorge Orta are our regular outfielders.

Miguel Dilone can't be kept on the bench all the time. So he splits some time with Joe. Joe is going to be a fine player. He'll improve. Right now, he is always a threat. If a pitcher makes a mistake, he jumps on him."

"Maybe if I was hitting like I know I can, I would be more upset," said Joe. "It's strange. In the Minors, I was a guess hitter. I'd think I was going to get a curve. When it came, I'd swing at it even if it was six inches off the ground. It worked for me. One of the home runs I hit came on a pitch I guessed at. It was low, but I hit it out anyway. I think I have to be more aggressive. I've been sitting back too much at the plate."

On the day he was batting his season's low, .264, Charboneau had two singles, a double, and drove in a run to lead the Indians to a 6–2 victory over the Minnesota Twins. A breakthrough of sorts occurred on the following day, June 14th. For the first time that season, Joe was penciled in to bat fourth.

"He's been doing the job," said Garcia. "And he's stopped trying to pull the ball. He's hitting the outside pitch to right. He's maturing."

There would be yet another surprise as Joe approached his 25th birthday on June 17th. Agent Dan Donnelly arranged to have Joe's mother, Kathleen, fly to Cleveland and see her son play a few games.

"The last two years, I hit home runs on my birthday," said Joe. "In fact, last year at this time I went 4-for-4 and was batting .404 at Chattanooga." This June 17th, however, Charboneau failed to get a hit in three trips against White Sox lefty Ken Kravec.

KANSAS CITY, MISSOURI, June 18 — Super Joe Charboneau and Kansas City catcher John Wathan nearly came to blows tonight in the Royals 10-2 victory over the Indians.

The heralded Charboneau temper, the one we'd heard and read about so much in the preceding months, came within a few syllables of erupting.

Fifth inning. The Indians were trailing 5–2. There were two outs, and Larry Gura, on the way to his ninth win, was pitching for the Royals. Gura had allowed just two hits until this point in the game, one of them being a weak single to left in the third inning by Super Joe.

The count was 1-and-2 when the Kansas City lefty fired a pitch that buzzed the rookie's batting helmet. As Joe was digging back into the batter's box, Royals catcher John Wathan said, "That's for looking at my signals. The kid was furious, and immediately began an eyeball-to-face-mask jawing with Wathan.

"I couldn't believe it," said Joe. "You'd have thought I had hit two home runs, not a cheap single. I was not looking at any signals. Sometimes when I am getting myself ready, I will look down to make sure I am set just right, but in no way do I look back. The thing that really burned me up was that when Gura threw at me, he didn't have the guts to come down and get involved in the argument."

Charboneau and Wathan were separated by home plate umpire Ken Kaiser. Fortunately, it was Kaiser behind the plate. At 230 pounds, he has a lot of weight to throw around if he needs to.

BLOOMINGTON, MINNESOTA, June 22 — Super Joe Charboneau had three hits, including a two-run home run, as the Indians defeated the Minnesota Twins, 11-6.

Joe Charboneau's tenth home run of the season was no gargantuan blast. It was a modest 355 feet in Metropolitan Stadium, the only baseball park which measures the distance of home runs and posts the results on the scoreboard almost instantaneously.

What made this home run unusual was that it was hit with a broken bat. A broken-bat hit is lucky to make it out of the infield. Joe's carried into the outfield grandstand. It was considered an awesome shot, even if the Twins pitcher was the immortal Fernando Arroyo, who will never be confused with Steve Carlton.

"I hit the ball right on the handle of the bat, and it broke," said Joe. "I'm really not that surprised that I hit it out. Each year, I usually break two bats on home runs."

True to form, he later had another broken-bat homer. This time the pitcher was Baltimore's Mike Flanagan.

The bat Joe smashed in his blow in Minnesota did not even belong to him. A player who spent much of the season using other players' bats, Joe had borrowed a Gary Alexander model to use against Arroyo.

Since Alexander was spending his season pouting on the bench, he had little use for his bats.

Alexander and Joe had become friends, however. Gary is an eloquent sort with an ego the size of the Goodyear Blimp. He is always more than willing to give advice, and Joe enjoyed listening to him. During this stretch, Charboneau was striking out more than ever before.

"Look, don't worry about it," said Alexander. "If you were to take all of Babe Ruth's strikeouts and string them together, he would have gone two seasons without hitting the ball."

Alexander is the E. F. Hutton of strikeouts. People listen when he discusses the subject. After all, he just missed a Major League record by fanning 166 times in 1978. That year, he was a regular and hit 27 homers, so the whiffs hardly bothered him. One sportswriter called him the GAS man, GAS standing for Gary Alexander Strikeouts.

CLEVELAND, OHIO, June 23 — The Indians traded Cliff Johnson to the Chicago Cubs for two players to be named later.

This drew but a few lines under the "transaction" column in most newspapers. It was a minor deal. Cliff Johnson was going to yet another new team. He is traded as often as Chevy Chase takes a fall. Furthermore, he was traded for not one, but two players to be named later. One of the indignities of baseball is to be traded for an unidentified player. The only thing worse is simply to be sold like a slave.

While most people greeted the Johnson move with a yawn, it meant a great deal to Joe Charboneau. Johnson had been the Indians designated hitter. His absence meant more playing time for Joe.

"We thought that Joe could do the job," said Indians Manager Dave Garcia. "That's why we traded Johnson. We thought that Cliff's presence made Joe feel as though he had to get hits all the time or he would be yanked out of the lineup."

The exit of Cliff Johnson brought an end to another minor legend with the Indians.

Johnson was obtained by the Tribe from the Yankees in June, 1979. He was dumped by New York for breaking the right thumb of Yankee relief pitcher Rich Gossage in a playful shower scuffle, and thus knocking him out for most of the year. Many feel the loss of Gossage enabled the Baltimore Orioles to beat out the Yankees for the American League pennant. In fact, the Oriole players jokingly said that Johnson deserved the Most Valuable Player Award for sidelining Gossage.

In 1979, destruction seemed to follow Cliff, as he collided with umpire Lou Dimuro while running to the plate. Dimuro spent six weeks in the hospital. In Cleveland, Johnson played like an All-Star, as he tends to do when first joining a new team. The 6′4″, 214-pound Texan hit 18 homers, drove in 61 runs and hit .271 for the Tribe in half a season. He was rewarded with a three-year, $500,000 contract by Indians President Gabe Paul for his efforts. After signing the contract, it is said that Paul told Cliff to go to the store and buy a new watch for himself, and charge it to the ballclub. A source close to Johnson said that the watch picked by Cliff sold for $2,000, a fact that did not exactly thrill Gabe Paul.

From the moment Cliff received his new contract, he ceased to be a productive player with the Indians.

Just before spring training, Johnson smashed the middle finger of his left hand, while unloading a barrel of oats off a truck at his San Antonio farm. Then he proceeded to spend most of spring training at his farm rather than on the field. Running the gamut of excuses for not working out, his absences earned him a $1,000 fine from Garcia. These antics did not surprise his teammates.

"Cliff Johnson is the laziest ballplayer I have ever seen," said one Indian, who has watched thousands. "A half-hour before the game, he would be sitting in the dugout smoking a cigarette and sipping from a cup of coffee. He never wanted to do anything."

Super Joe and Cliff seemed to get along quite well, however.

"I called him 'The Old Man,'" said Joe. "He was so big, and he always acted like he was mad so people would be afraid of him. I kind of liked him once I figured him out. He was fun to talk to."

A memory of the 1980 season that stays with Joe is of a Johnson home run at Fenway Park. With one out in the ninth, the Indians were trailing Boston, 2–0. Charboneau singled and moved to second on a Rick Manning base hit. Rookie Jerry Dybzinski was the next batter, but Dave Garcia decided to use Johnson as a pinch hitter. Johnson was drinking coffee in the clubhouse, however, as he had thought he would not see any action, when he received the call to bat.

"I was on second base when Cliff came up to bat," said Joe. "I couldn't believe what I was seeing. He was standing at the plate without his spikes. He was wearing tennis shoes."

Johnson worked Boston pitcher Chuck Rainey to a count of two balls and two strikes. Then he lifted a towering home run over the Green Monster in left field, and the Indians went on to win 3–2.

This time, Johnson did not heave the bat after he swung, which is part of the Johnson mystique. Seldom did the big man swing without someone having to duck out of the way of his flying bat. No one throws a bat more than Cliff Johnson, who also kisses it before he steps up to the plate. Maybe there is a relationship?

Charboneau's friendship with Cliff did have a stormy side. Early in the season, Johnson was on third base. Ron Hassey hit a sacrifice fly. Never a sprinter, Johnson tagged up at third and lumbered toward the plate. The on-deck hitter was Joe, and he motioned for Cliff to slide. Johnson hit the dirt. The throw was wide of the plate. It was generally agreed that Cliff could have scored without the benefit of a slide.

Cliff never likes to use any extra effort, and he was enraged at Charboneau for telling him to slide. He berated the rookie, and the argument continued after Joe took his turn at the plate and returned to the dugout. Momentarily, it appeared that the two huge men were about to slug it out, before order was restored.

Later, Joe dismissed the happening as nothing, but added, "You have to stand up for your rights. You can't let anyone push you around if you want respect."

"That was nothing," Johnson said of the incident. "Joe is a good kid."

On the field, the Indians were not exactly an artistic success. Their record was 33–33. A 13–3 loss to Detroit, in which four Tribe pitchers walked 14 Tigers, had dropped the Indians to the .500 mark.

Meanwhile, a man who called himself Hal Symons from *Rolling Stone* magazine joined the Indians on the road. He was an odd fellow, but friendly and intelligent. He seldom took notes and did not carry a typewriter, which made some wonder if he was indeed a writer. It turned out that he was a disbarred lawyer and con-man. He never worked for

Rolling Stone, but he kept the scam going for three weeks, in which he made two trips with the team and ran up $900 worth of bills. He said he was with the Indians to do a story on the baseball strike and one about Super Joe Charboneau.

NEW YORK CITY, NEW YORK, June 28 — Indians rookie Super Joe Charboneau came within three feet of becoming the first player to hit a fair ball into the third deck of the remodeled Yankee Stadium.

Joe Charboneau added a new wrinkle to his legend before the largest press corps that had ever witnessed him perform. It was the third inning of the Indians game with the Yankees when Charboneau unloaded on a 3-and-1 fastball from New York left-hander Tom Underwood. The ball left the park as if it was launched from Cape Canaveral. Joe stood at home plate and marveled at his shot, in a fine imitation of New York slugger Reggie Jackson. The ball returned to earth and struck the facing of the third deck, about 599 feet from home plate.

"It is a weird feeling when you hit a ball that well," said Joe. "It is almost as though you don't feel it, because you have hit it so squarely. You are numb, floating on air."

The renovated Yankee Stadium was reopened in 1976. No player had reached the third deck in fair territory. Veteran Yankee broadcaster Phil Rizzuto can only recall two balls hit into the third deck in the old Yankee Stadium. One came off the bat of 6′ 7″ Frank Howard and the other was hit by Jimmie Foxx.

This was Charboneau's initial visit to the famed Yankee Stadium. He had heard of the monuments behind the centerfield fence honoring Babe Ruth, Lou Gehrig and Miller Huggins, but a personal superstition prevented him from taking a close look at them.

"I get funny about certain things like the monuments," said Joe. "Something inside me said that I should not go out and look at them, or I would jinx myself. Maybe I will check them out when my career is over."

Perhaps this reluctance evolved from an earlier superstition. The Indians were playing the White Sox, and they were on the bus that would carry them from their Chicago hotel to Comiskey Park. On the journey along Michigan Avenue, there were several large monuments. One of them featured a huge lion.

"Whatever you do," Indians third baseman Toby Harrah told Joe, "Don't look at the lion's balls when we go by."

"Why not?" asked Joe.

"You don't want to know," said Harrah.

"Tell me," said Joe.

"Because it's bad luck," said Harrah.

"When we got to the statue I couldn't help but look," said Joe. "This year I had only two hits in Chicago. One was a bleeder off the handle and the other was a broken bat hit. I'll never look at the lion's balls again."

On the road, Charboneau had a few bizarre encounters. Especially, it seemed, in New York.

"There are too many crazies in that town," said Joe. "I was at this bar having a drink, and this girl comes up to me and asks me to dance. I don't dance so I told her, no. Later, I found out that it wasn't a girl at all, but it was a guy in a dress. New York is a wild place. I remember walking around on Seventh Avenue after a night game, and seeing a guy wearing a space suit walk by. No one but me seemed to think it was strange."

19 ★★★★
★★★★

PUNK ROCK

CLEVELAND, OHIO, July 13 — The largest crowd of the 1980 Major League baseball season, 73,096, watched Wayne Garland shut out the Yankees while giving up only two hits. Super Joe Charboneau drove in four runs on three hits as the Cleveland Indians downed New York, 7–0.

This was the Indians' largest crowd since opening day of 1973, when 74,420 packed Cleveland Stadium. They saw the ghosts of the Indians' past and future put it all together for one glorious evening.

On the mound was Wayne Garland, a man whose right arm had been pronounced dead. He was pitching for a team many said needed the last rites, too.

They called Wayne Garland the Indians $2.3 million mistake. The Tribe gave him a ten-year contract worth that amount before the 1977 season. Then he was struck with a rotator-cuff injury to his right shoulder. To a pitcher, that is the obituary, the final curtain. No hurler has ever rebounded from that injury. It has finished the likes of Don Gullett and Steve Busby.

But in 1980, Garland made a comeback. Certainly, he did not approach the form of 1976, when he was a 20-game winner for the

Orioles, but he was pitching again, when most said it was time for him to take up selling insurance. This man and his once maligned arm gave the beleaguered town of Cleveland a reason to feel good. They beat the Yankees, the best club money could buy. What made it even better was that the New York Yankees, owned by former Clevelander, George Steinbrenner, were on their way to another division title.

This July evening was like Cleveland baseball during the winning years of the 1940s and 1950s. It was a night when the fans came to say they were for Cleveland and there was nothing wrong with that.

It was on this night that Joe Charboneau discovered what it would be like to play for a winner in Cleveland. The mob came to see the Yankees and what was advertised as "the world's greatest fireworks show." They would gladly return for a successful Indians team.

"I love big crowds," said Joe. "They get me so jacked up, I feel like hitting one out every time I bat."

Charboneau was given a standing ovation for his two singles and a double. Garland received the same. An extrovert, Joe had no qualms about stepping out of the dugout and waving his cap to the cheering throng. Garland seemed uncomfortable in front of the people, who saw his first shutout in three years.

"This had to rate as perhaps the most satisfying game I have ever pitched," said Garland, whose gruff nature earned him the nickname Grumpy. "I was really nervous. It is not every day that I pitch against the Yankees in front of 73,000 people."

Garland went 3–8 after his victory over the Yankees and finished the year with a 6–9 record and a 4.61 ERA. It is still too early to tell if he is back, but it was not too soon for the Cleveland papers to continue building the legend of Super Joe. They heralded Charboneau's ability to respond before huge crowds, using his opening day performance as an example. Again, they compared him to Rocky Colavito and discussed his bright future.

After the win over the Yankees, the Indians and Joe slumped in the remaining four games before the All-Star break. Charboneau finished the first half with a .291 batting average, 11 homers and 42 RBIs, despite not hitting safely in his last 13 at bats.

But his popularity continued to soar. This was demonstrated when a couple of local baseball fans, Don Kriss and Stan Bloch, released a record which reached the top of the pop charts. It was called, "Go Joe Charboneau." That was also the refrain, which was said in a primal chant that almost resembled a grunt because of the heavy beat by a group called The Section 36 Singers.

"It's a punk rock song and I'm a punk rock ballplayer," said Joe.

The words to "Go Joe Charboneau" are these:

> Who's the newest guy in town?
> He's turned the ballpark upside down.
> *Chorus:* Go Joe Charboneau
> Who do we appreciate?
> Fits right in with the other eight.
> *Chorus:* Go Joe Charboneau
>
> Who's the one to keep our hopes alive?
> From spring through the summer to the pennant drive?
> *Chorus:* Go Joe Charboneau
> So raise your glass, let out a cheer,
> For Cleveland's Rookie of the Year.
> *Chorus:* Go Joe Charboneau

From the record, Joe donated the $1,000 proceeds to Our Lady of the Wayside Home for handicapped children. There was more Super Joe hype. A poster released by a company called "The Spot" showed a bare-chested Joe Charboneau wearing a cape and a straw cowboy hat. In the middle of his stomach was a circle with the words "The Spot."

"I'm not so sure about the poster," said Joe. "I'm a little embarrassed by it. I don't have the face for it. This is the first time I have combed my hair to play baseball. Now, if they could put Duane Kuiper's head on my body, we could sell underwear."

More than 5,000 posters were sold at $3 each. You can be sure that the 350 members of the Joe Charboneau fan club played a big part in the sales. They would sit in Section 36, which was behind left field. Joe's fan club is the largest in the 80-year history of the Indians. But the publicity did not faze Joe. Dan Donnelly had helped him purchase some impressive clothes, and he was a hit with the media and the fans. Joe was still his own man, however, as he drove a 1955 pickup truck to the park each day. The truck was about to be junked by Donnelly's heating business, before Charboneau salvaged it.

"The publicity makes me feel good," said Joe. "I enjoy it. I have been taking a lot of ribbing from my teammates and the visiting players, but it is fun."

Over the All-Star break, Charboneau also discovered a new game. Promoters of two Cleveland-area golf tournaments convinced him to try his swing on the links. He had never teed up.

On the first day, he lost 18 balls during his trip over the 18-hole course. Joe lined a ball so hard against a tree that a piece of bark fell off. The second day saw him lose 15 balls, but he finished the day down just three, as he won a dozen golf balls in a drawing. During this round, Joe sliced a shot so badly off the tee that it put a hole through his partner's golf bag. A disbelieving fan retrieved the ball and asked Charboneau to autograph it.

Most of the Indians' better golfers would not play with Joe after hearing the tales of his ridiculous aim. Donnelly introduced him to Ed Fitzgerald, a scratch golfer, and lessons began. Six weeks later, Joe played nine holes with Fitzgerald and Indians Pitcher Sandy Wihtol in which Charboneau carded a 48.

20

AFTER THE ALL-STAR BREAK

TORONTO, CANADA, July 11 — Joe Charboneau's batting average dips to .286 as he goes hitless in four at bats. The Indians lose, 6–3, to Toronto.

The slump that began right before the All-Star break came back stronger than ever after the season paused for three days. Joe was on a 1-for-21 skid. He was beginning to think about it. And he was thinking too much and about the wrong things. He had convinced himself that he could not hit on astroturf, especially the surface in Toronto. He went to Manager Dave Garcia and told him so. For obvious reasons, Garcia was wondering about Super Joe.

"If a guy has it in his head that he can't hit in a certain park or off certain pitchers, then he won't," said Garcia, who again was baffled by the attitudes of what he called "the modern ballplayer."

Dan Donnelly was in Toronto to view the series. He heard and saw what was happening to Joe. Over dinner, he told Charboneau that it was time for him to grow up and quit making excuses. He reminded Joe that he would not have made the team if it weren't for the injury to Andre Thornton, and that he had better straighten out or he would be playing in the Pacific Coast League. Initially, Joe did not take the advice well, as he smashed a glass on the floor because of his frustration with himself.

"The reason Joe got upset was that Dan had hit home with him," said Cindy. "He simmered down soon after breaking the glass and realized that Dan was right. He had to stop making excuses."

"In dealing with Joe at times like these, I would say things to bring him back down, and then I would build him up," said Donnelly. "After he realized the reasons for his slump, he and I would then talk about what to do to get out of it. That is what we did in Toronto. During hard times, I remind him of the highlights of the year, where he had come through on big days like opening day."

"Dan was very good at keeping Joe on an even keel," said Kathleen Charboneau. "To me, Dan Donnelly was an answer to my prayers. He was not afraid to be honest with Joe when he needed it, yet he would not ruin Joe's confidence."

"Everyone tends to think that Joe is this big tough guy," said Cindy. "In some respects, he is. But he worries about failing. There were nights when he would come home and cry because he thought he wouldn't cut it. This was a very difficult time for him."

Like most baseball wives, Cindy Charboneau was not immune to her husband's moods.

"I received a lot of help from the Indians' wives," said Cindy. "We would talk about the bad times, and it was nice to know that we all went through the same thing at one point or another. Wives all feel what we call 'baseball problems,' which happens when the team or your husband isn't doing well."

ARLINGTON, TEXAS, July 14 — Super Joe was benched for the first two games of the series and then returned to the lineup, going 0-for-4 as the Indians lost, 4–2, to the Texas Rangers.

The slump was now 1-for-26. The batting average was .282. Joe was sliding right out of the Major Leagues, and he knew it. Instead of looking in the mirror, he was blaming everything else for his demise.

In the sixth inning of a game with the Rangers, Charboneau fanned weakly on three fastballs from Texas's Danny Darwin. Ironically,

Darwin had also fanned Joe in his first professional at bat, as a member of the Spartanburg Phillies in 1976.

After going down this time against Darwin, Joe walked back to the dugout. He was about 30 feet from Garcia when he muttered at the manager, "Why didn't you bench me for a couple more games after the three-day All-Star break?"

The newspapers were calling Joe "super," but that did not give him the right to challenge a manager's decision. Certainly not midway through his rookie year, while the manager had spent 40 years in the game. But that was not the reason Charboneau found himself on the bench during the next three games. When the Tribe dropped four of five games after the All-Star break, the Indians front office was in a frenzy. The team wasn't hitting, and something had to be done, if for no other reason than to make it look as though the men in charge were trying to correct the situation.

So the Indians recalled designated hitter Gary Gray from their Tacoma farm club. Gray was hitting .335 and leading the Pacific Coast League with 20 home runs and 73 RBI.

"We need a hot bat," said Indians President Gabe Paul. "That's why we called up Gray."

"When Gray joined the team, I knew that I wasn't going to play much," said Joe. "Since Cliff Johnson had been traded, I had been the DH. Now Gray would fill that role, and that left me the odd man out."

In his first game as a Cleveland Indian, Gray went 2-for-3 with a home run. The 27-year-old Louisiana native had never hit less than .300 in seven Minor League seasons. He was determined to stick in the Majors this time, after three previously unsuccessful tries.

Finishing the Texas series, the Tribe flew to play three games in Anaheim. Art Charboneau had come to southern California to visit his son. He had not seen Joe play since their year together in Portland in 1970. Joe went to Garcia and asked if the manager would let him perform in front of his father.

"Gary Alexander and Alan Bannister had relatives in California and I know that they went to Dave and he played them," said Joe. "But I sat through the three games. This was the first time I had ever asked a manager if I could play. Garcia said that he couldn't play everyone who asked. At that point, I was really down. I felt that Dave was trying to rub my nose in the ground."

What bothered Joe was that he was not the only Indian in a slump. Gray's home run had been the first for the Indians in 13 games. Several other players were not hitting, yet they remained in the lineup.

"I like to play through my slumps," said Joe. "That is what I did in the Minors. I have gone 1-for-48 and then gotten hot."

"Joe just wasn't swinging well," said Garcia. "He had an excellent season going and he will be a fine Major League hitter, but he has to learn to handle the times when he doesn't hit. He can't get so down that those 0-for-8s turns into 0-for-25s."

In Oakland, more than 200 friends and relatives of Charboneau showed up to watch him play. It seemed like most of nearby Santa Clara was at Oakland Coliseum to see their native son. Several Joe Charboneau groups were welcomed to the park by the public-address announcer. Meanwhile, Joe batted once in three games and popped out. He had been at bat just five times in the Indians' last eight games.

Soon, like the rest of the Indians, Gary Gray was no longer hitting. The team batted .132 in three straight losses to Oakland, and the Indians were 4–7 since the All-Star break. The season's record had dropped to 41–46, and Charboneau, the man who still led the club in homers and RBIs, was on the bench. Garcia was being criticized for this tactic.

The next stop on the trip was Seattle, and Joe returned to the lineup and was hitless again, making his slump 1-for-31. Garcia played him again the next day and the Indians won 4–0 behind the pitching of Len Barker. The offensive leader was Charboneau, who had three hits. It now appeared that Garcia was going to use Joe primarily against left-handed pitchers. He had a .420 batting average vs. southpaws and .230 vs. right-handers.

SEATTLE, WASHINGTON, July 23 — Joe Charboneau hit two home runs, one of them with the bases loaded, to drive in six runs as the Indians defeated Seattle, 12–6.

Joe's last home run had been a month ago in New York, the shot off the facing of the third deck. It also signaled a slide in his production and his eventual benching.

During the last month, Charboneau had often walked about like a zombie. Not playing, and not hitting when he did get into a game, coated him with depression. Even though his fan mail was 100 percent supportive and the Cleveland newspapers clamored for Joe to be presented the opportunity to play through his slumps, Charboneau remained in the dumps. During this period, Indians' Coach Joe Nossek spent a good deal of time talking with the rookie, in hopes of rebuilding his confidence.

"The first time I saw Joe, there was something special about him," said Nossek. "He has one of those nice friendly smiles that makes you feel like you have known him all your life. He has certain qualities that make me think he was born to be great."

The Nossek-Charboneau discussions would always conclude with a smile. On this night in Seattle, Joe found himself in the lineup. Nossek, the Tribe's third base coach, and Joe were saying that they were happy the Indians were finally coming to the close of the 14-day trip. Then Charboneau said, "The next time I hit a home run, I'm going to give you a kiss while rounding third base." Both men laughed.

It was the third inning of the game. With Ron Hassey on first base, Seattle pitcher Jim Beattie delivered a fat fastball which Joe sent flying 420 feet into the left field seats. As his home run trot carried him to second base, Charboneau broke into a grin. Touching third, Joe reached out to plant the promised kiss on Nossek. Smiling, Nossek backed away and suggested that Joe save his kisses for Cindy.

Nine innings later, the Indians and Mariners were still playing. They were locked in a 5–5 contest when the Tribe erupted like nearby Mt. Saint Helens. They scored seven times, and the key hit was the first Major League grand-slam homer by Super Joe. This time, Joe saw that Nossek was looking as though he was ready to kiss the rookie as he rounded the bases. Again, both men were in hysterics.

A few weeks earlier, Charboneau had caused Nossek some pain and given him a limp. Joe ripped a liner off Nossek's left ankle. The foul ball struck Nossek while he was standing in the third base coach's box, and it left him with a foot that was purple, blue and swollen to the size of a grapefuit.

Interestingly, Joe's Seattle slam would be the last home run he would hit on the road in 1980. His final 10 would come in Cleveland.

CLEVELAND, OHIO, July 26 — Super Joe Charboneau's three-run homer powered the Indians to a 10–2 victory over California.

Joe had long predicted a hot streak.

"Whenever I go into slumps, I come out in a big way," said Joe. "In Chattanooga, I once hit two grand slams in four days. At Visalia, I went eight straight games in which I had at least three hits. When I get into these streaks, I feel like I can hit anyone or any pitch."

In his last three games, Charboneau had three homers and nine RBIs.

"I get very superstitious when I'm going good," said Joe. "I will stay with the same bat and the same batting glove, no matter how ripped up the glove may get. When I'm hot, I will drink the same flavor of soft drink and put my uniform on the same way. When I'm not hitting, I'm breaking out new batting gloves every day, and I'll never use the old ones again."

Prior to each game, Joe also slips a plastic four-leaf clover into his pocket. He received the charm from Margaret Engle, his mother-in-law. Joe wears a Mother of Perpetual Help medal round his neck. He also considered the 1955 pickup truck lucky, until the brakes gave out one day and he narrowly avoided a collision with a Cadillac.

Charboneau's super streak continued the following day, as he went 3-for-3 with four RBIs. His .565 batting average with three homers and 14 RBIs would net him American League Player of the Week honors.

But the streak would end right after being named the Player of the Week, as he jammed his left hand while making a diving catch in left field.

"I hurt it so badly that I thought it was broken," said Joe, who missed only two games because of the injury. At this point, he was batting .299 with 14 homers and 57 RBIs.

CLEVELAND, OHIO, August 4 — Joe Charboneau, Jorge Orta,

*Rick Manning and Bo Diaz homered as the Indians beat the
Toronto Blue Jays, 11–5.*

There was nothing spectacular about Joe's 16th homer of the season.
It was just a line drive over the left field fence. "That one was special to
me," said Joe.

Before each home game, Joe usually will sign autographs for the fans
near the Indians dugout. He will spend 30 minutes with the fans, which
is more time than most of the Indians players. It is also a reason that he
is the team's most popular athlete.

"I like meeting the fans, and I don't mind signing autographs," said
Charboneau. "What makes me feel bad is that I can't sign everybody's
or I would be signing autographs all day. I know that when I go out to
sign, I am going to end up disappointing some people by not having
enough time to get to them. That bothers me."

It is not uncommon for Joe to toss balls into the stands to fans during
batting practice. This earned him a few reprimands from the Indians
front office, because they did not want any fans to be injured while
scrambling for the balls. During his personal appearances, he tells
children to give him their names and addresses and he will send them
Super Joe T-shirts or baseballs. The slips of paper then go to Donnelly, who fills the requests with Joe paying for the free souvenirs.

Joe also purchases batting helmets and other Indians souvenirs, and
distributes them to children at hospitals and at other charity affairs.

"Joe would give up the shirt off his back," said Joe Nossek.

Charboneau has told several friends that one of his goals is to earn
enough money so he can open up an orphanage or a home for handi-
capped children.

"When Joe does a personal appearance, he almost always stays
longer than his alloted time so he can make sure to sign everyone's
autograph and talk to the fans," said Donnelly. "Every time we get a
charity request, he wants to do it. But we get fifteen to twenty a week,
and we can't do them all."

Before this game with the Blue Jays, Joe spotted a girl with braces on
her legs. She wanted Charboneau's autograph.

"I'm glad to do it," said Charboneau, who then found a baseball for the girl. As he signed the ball, the little girl said, "Would you hit a home run for me?"

"I wasn't even thinking when I said okay," said Joe. "Afterwards, I began to think about what I had said. I shouldn't promise things that I can't deliver. That made me really want to hit one out for her."

In the second inning, Joe faced Toronto southpaw Paul Mirabella. Joe lined Mirabella's first pitch into the left field seats.

"The first thing I thought of when I hit the ball was the little girl," said Joe. "I was so happy for her."

Charboneau would later learn that the girl was suffering from spina bifida, a birth defect of the spinal cord. Because of that little girl, Joe became interested in her plight. He became the local chairman of the Spina Bifida Association, and will be making appearances to raise money for the foundation.

The home run against Mirabella was the second time Joe had kept such a promise.

"When Dan Donnelly's first daughter, Meredith, was born, I told Dan that I would hit a home run that night," said Joe, who did connect against Baltimore's Mike Flanagan that evening.

"I try not to get myself in the habit of promising home runs," said Joe. "But now and then I can't help but say yes."

CLEVELAND, OHIO, August 16 — Super Joe Charboneau hit his 17th home run as the Indians dropped a 10-5 decision to the Milwaukee Brewers.

For Joe, there was no celebrating after this game. Not only had his home run proven to be meaningless, in the pasting by Milwaukee, but he had again pulled his groin muscle. It was the same muscle which sidelined him for the final six weeks of the 1979 season at Chattanooga, and it was the same muscle which acted up and helped speed Joe's return from winter ball in Mexico.

"It had been bothering me several times during the year," said Joe. "I especially felt it when we played on artificial turf, in places like Seattle, Toronto and Kansas City. Running in those parks really tore me up.

Because of the surface, ground balls get through the infield faster. It makes it easier to hit, but my legs hurt me too much when I play there."

Charboneau is fortunate that he did not make the Majors as a member of the Phillies. Philadelphia is in the National League, and it is one of six stadiums in that loop with artificial surfaces. Grass prevails in all but three of the 14 American League parks.

Despite his injury, Joe was in the lineup again for the next game. This time, it was his ears which ended up hurting. It had finally happened. Cleveland booed its favorite son after he failed to run down a fly ball.

"I deserved it," said Joe. "I had been waiting for the boos to come, and in a way, I am glad it did happen. I was booed before in the Minors, and there is no way you can go through a season without catching some boos. I wasn't surprised by what happened. At that point of the season, the fans were booing everyone but their own mothers."

Booing is as much a part of recent Indians' history as sixth place. Give the town a lousy team, and the fans usually stay away. Those who do show up tend to fall into two categories. First are those who love the game and would never imagine booing anyone under any circumstances. They are the purists, who like to see the Indians win, but more important, want to see a solid game played by both teams.

Then there are those who bring all their frustrations to the stadium and heave them out on the players in a strange Freudian manner. They blame the floundering ballclub for their personal failures. Booing is an art to them. They boo everyone, but one player each year is usually singled out for special abuse. In the past, one of their targets was Buddy Bell. In 1980, Rick Manning bore the brunt of the criticism.

At 25, Manning, considered a gifted defensive centerfielder, was in the midst of a rough season.

"I thought some of the stuff Rick took was vicious," said Charboneau. "Rick and I would talk about it. He said that you can't let that stuff get to you. He said it never bothered him, and I never heard him complain. But being booed all the time has to hurt. One day, he said to me that the Cleveland fans used to cheer him like they cheer me now. That made me stop and think."

Manning joined the Indians when he was 20. During his rookie year, he played the game with such enthusiasm that it seemed impossible for anyone to try harder or hustle more than Rick Manning. He batted .285 as a rookie and then .292 in his second year.

"During that time, Rick Manning was the one ballplayer I would pay to watch play," said Dave Garcia.

"There will come a time when a .300 batting average and 40 stolen bases will be a poor season for Rick," said Frank Robinson, who managed Manning during his rookie season.

At 20, Manning was aware of the dangers in front of him.

"I know that drinking, women and an inflated ego can lead to mediocrity," said Manning. "I know that getting a big head means getting lazy. I have the choice of going that way or not."

In his first two years, Manning appeared ready to turn Frank Robinson into a prophet.

"I love the crowd," Manning said after his second season. "I feel I am there to put on a show for the fans, who spend their hard-earned money to watch the games. If I give 100 percent, I feel good and the fans sense it. I'll be a hot dog, but I'll never be a dog."

Then came the problems.

A broken back turned the 1978 season into a lost year. In between, he had received a five-year, $1.5 million contract from the Indians in 1978 when a legal snafu by the ballclub gave Manning the same excellent bargaining position as a free agent. At 23, Manning became a million-aire, and the fans resented his wealth. When his offensive production and intensity faltered, the Indians' followers were waiting for an opportunity to make Manning the scapegoat for everything that was wrong with the franchise.

In the waning days of the year, Manning would wear a T-shirt which said, I SURVIVED THE 1980 BASEBALL SEASON. Even though Rick hit the ball hard all year, the hits just wouldn't fall in for him.

A glance at Manning's career is enough to make Charboneau know that nothing is guaranteed. It all can go so wrong so fast. People change and success slips away. It is the old show-business adage about the crowd loving you one day and booing you the next. The fans ask only one question: "What have you done for me today?" If the answer is "nothing," they forget you exist, or what you did in the past.

"That kind of stuff can be scary if you think about it," said Charboneau. "I know that I have to work and be very careful. I like what I have going right now, and I want to keep it."

21 ★★★★★★★★

INJURY

CHICAGO, ILLINOIS, August 21 — Dan Spillner hurled a one-hitter as the Indians downed the Chicago White Sox, 3–0.

Joe's groin problems had turned him into a full-time designated hitter. It also seemed to bring him closer to Dave Garcia. Garcia was very impressed by Joe's willingness to stay in the lineup despite his painful injury.

Some had suggested that Garcia did not show Charboneau enough compassion and patience when he slumped, but these troubles appeared to be over.

"I think I was right in keeping Joe out of the lineup when he stopped hitting," said Garcia. "But there were times when I kept him out too long. Maybe I should have taken him out earlier and then put him back in sooner. When I sat him down, I wanted to rest his head. After he hit that home run on opening day and then everybody was calling him Super Joe, I think he tried to hit a home run every time, and he pressed too much. Then he started making excuses. But he has grown up over the course of the season. He is an outstanding hitter, and I don't remember a rookie with his discipline at the plate."

"It took me a while to get used to Garcia," said Joe. "I found out that

it is not his way to talk to rookies. He had nothing against me person-
ally. By the end of the year, we were talking a lot, and I came to respect
him as a manager and as a man. I feel very good about playing for him."

On the night of Spillner's one-hitter, Joe was serving as the DH.
Spillner worked the game of his life, missing baseball immortality by
two outs, as Chicago's Leo Sutherland broke up his no-hit bid with a
ninth inning single between shortstop and third base.

"The last no-hitter I saw was in high school," said Joe. "It was a
seven-inning job, and I didn't even know what was happening until the
last inning, when the coach told me to dive for anything that came my
way in right field. Then I got really excited, but nothing was hit to me."

Charboneau was just one of several ballplayers on edge as Spillner
went for the no-hitter.

"Everybody was pulling hard for him," said Joe. "Even the Chicago
fans wanted him to get it. They were cheering for Spillner and booed the
White Sox when they got the hit. Man, Comiskey Park is a wild place."

Playing or watching a baseball game in Chicago is an experience in
itself. At Comiskey Park, you can purchase hard liquor at one of the
several bars. Then you are eased into the flow of the game by the best
and liveliest organist in baseball. He could rev up a crowd of corpses
into a wild mob. Finally, you have to dodge a goon squad that is
tougher than the men guarding Frank Sinatra.

The booze is the catalyst for the wild nights on Chicago's South Side
ballpark. By the sixth inning, fights break out across the park and it is
not uncommon for players to toss up towels into the grandstands as an
aid to a fan who just had his face bloodied. While the brawls are painful
to the participants, the fighters often find themselves battered even more
when "help" arrives. A group of about 50 men, who resemble large
rotund bouncers, circulate in the stands. They wear yellow windbreak-
ers which say "Sox Security Force" on the back, and they are not
adverse to tossing around their weight to restore order.

In the middle of this is Harry Caray. He is a man with a gruff voice
who is a guru to White Sox fans. He broadcasts the club's games both
on the radio and television, and his style is like that of a butcher. He rips
both the home team and the visitors with merciless, yet gleeful abandon.

For the most part, Charboneau's relationship with the media reflected his nickname.

"Everyone was nice to me," said Super Joe. "In fact, there were times when I thought I should have been criticized more than I was. I have never had problems with reporters. In fact, some of my favorite people are Nev Chandler, Herb Score, Bruce Drennan and Joe Tait, who are the Indians' announcers."

CLEVELAND, OHIO, August 26 — Mike Hargrove recorded his 1,000th Major League hit in the Indians 5-1 loss to the Minnesota Twins.

Joe Charboneau spent much of the year batting behind Mike Hargrove.

"He gives you plenty of time to loosen up," said Charboneau. "Hargrove is something else."

Dudley Michael Hargrove comes away with a single impression. Sure, he is a .300 hitter, and he walks 100 times a year. So do a few other players, but none of them take as long to finish their business at the plate as Mike.

Hargrove has been called everything from hyperactive to the human rain-delay. All he does is adjust his helmet, hitch up his pants, wipe the sweat off his forehead, pull on his shirt sleeves, pull the batting glove down over his right thumb and wipe sweat from his upper lip. And he only goes through this routine after every pitch. Hargrove at bat is a signal for the fans to walk to the washroom, because they know he will just be stepping up when they return.

"If what I do bothers the pitchers, that's great," said Hargrove. "Baseball games are three hours long, anyhow, so five extra minutes for me doesn't hurt anything."

As the season progressed, Charboneau tended to follow Hargrove's example. Super Joe would not be given a speeding ticket for his approach to home plate, either.

"Like Hargrove, I have a pattern," said Joe. "On the way to the plate, I always walk around behind the umpire. Then I make the sign of the cross before I step into the box. Next, I take three practice swings, scrape the ground in the batter's box eight times with my right foot and twice with my left. Then I tap each spike shoe with the bat and then look down to the third base coach."

Three days after Hargrove's 1,000th hit, Donnelly surprised Joe by bringing his mother in from Santa Clara for a visit.

"I was so happy to see her," said Joe, who demonstrated it by hitting home runs in each of his next three games.

"Seeing his mother always turns Joe around," said Donnelly. "It is one of the best ways to cure his slumps."

BOSTON, MASSACHUSETTS, September 8 — The Indians hit into six doubleplays as they were crushed by Boston, 10–4.

Charboneau's ailing groin muscle grew progressively worse with each game. He had reached the point where he could do little more than walk down the baseline after hitting the ball. He was in and out of the lineup, depending upon the condition of the muscle. In Boston, Joe was one of the six doubleplay victims, and it was now clear that the Indians were on an unstoppable slide into sixth place.

Five days later, in Detroit, Joe pulled some stomach muscles while forcing his aching upper legs to run to first base.

"I knew I was in really bad shape after that," said Joe. "I had been to ten or twenty doctors, and no one was sure exactly what was wrong. All they knew was that the groin area was not right. At this point, I was starting to worry about my career. I thought I might need surgery or something. I was willing to do anything that would make it better."

Joe would start only one more game in 1980. The rest of his appearances would be in the pinch-hitting capacity.

That final start was September 17 in Boston. In the previous game, Red Sox rookie Dave Stapleton went 5-for-5 as the Indians were clobbered, 9–5. Stapleton had emerged as Joe's primary contender for the Rookie of the Year honors. Stapleton is a skinny, 6-0, 175-pound second baseman. He had been released by Boston and later re-signed when they needed an extra Minor League infielder. Like Joe, he had not been considered a top prospect until late in his Minor League career.

Charboneau was batting .287, with 22 homers and 84 RBIs at the time, compared to .323 with 7 home runs and 40 RBIs for Stapleton.

"I think that Stapleton is the top rookie," said Red Sox Manager Don Zimmer. "Charboneau has hit some home runs, but he is just a designated hitter. Stapleton plays the field every day, and he is a fine second baseman. I don't think there is that much of a choice."

"It is not fair to say that Joe is only a DH," said Dave Garcia, who supported his rookie to the Nth degree late in the season. "He is a respectable outfielder, and the only reason he is not playing the field is that he is hurt. Joe has worked hard and reached the point where he is one of our better defensive outfielders. He has good hands and his arm has improved."

Charboneau tried to stay out of the controversy between himself and Stapleton. He claimed that talking about the award had hindered his performance.

"I'm not going to pay any more attention to the rookie award," said Joe.

But watching Stapleton rap out five hits and reading the Boston newspapers pushing him for Rookie of the Year bothered Charboneau. The next day, Joe went to Dave Garcia and told the manager that he was well enough to play. Garcia wrote his name in the lineup. Joe fanned in his first three at bats, then he grounded out and finished off the miserable day by hitting into a doubleplay.

"It was obvious that Joe was not well enough to play," said Garcia. "I made a mistake by putting him in there."

"I was just so sick of sitting," said Joe, who also admitted that he desperately wanted to win the award. "I told Cindy during spring training that I would win the award for her if I got a chance to play. At that time, I knew I was so close to winning it that it really bothered me not being able to play."

CLEVELAND, OHIO, September 26 — Joe Charboneau ripped a pinch-hit home run to give the Indians a 5-4 victory over the Baltimore Orioles.

This would be Joe's most gratifying day of the 1980 season. It began with his father, Art Charboneau, visiting Joe. Art Charboneau had not

watched his son play since their year together in Portland. He came to
see Joe when the Indians were in Anaheim, but Joe was exiled to the
bench for that three-game series with the Angels.

Joe took his father with him to the game, and the two men spent a
long time sitting in the Indians clubhouse. Before the game began, Art
took a seat in the stands and saw his son honored as the most popular
Indians player for the 1980 season. The 6,362 fans gave Joe a standing
ovation as he walked off with a trophy.

Charboneau had mentioned to Dave Garcia that his father was in the
stands. He wanted to start.

"You and I both know that you aren't well enough to start," said
Garcia. "I don't want to risk you getting a more serious injury. But I will
find a spot for you to pinch-hit."

That opportunity came with one out in the seventh inning. The
Orioles had a 2–0 lead, and the Indians had a runner on first base.
Garcia sent Joe up to bat for Rick Manning. The pitcher was Mike
Flanagan, the 1979 Cy Young Award-winner.

"Hit the ball to the outfield grass," said Garcia to Charboneau. "I
don't want you hitting into a doubleplay."

As Joe took his practice swings, Cindy told Art Charboneau that he
would hit a home run.

Flanagan worked the count to two balls and two strikes on Super
Joe. Then Flanagan fired a fastball, and Joe sent it into the upper deck
in left field. It was the first time anyone reached the Cleveland Stadium
upper deck in 1980.

As Joe rounded the bases, Art Charboneau cried. After the game, he
waited for Joe outside the dressing room. When Joe came through the
door, he presented his father with the baseball he had hit for the home
run.

Over the course of the season, Joe paid for visits from his youngest
brother, John, his mother and father. All totaled, Joe spent about
$3,000 so his relatives could watch him play in Cleveland.

Art Charboneau was especially thrilled by his son's current lofty
status as a Major League ballplayer. This was demonstrated when Joe
and his dad passed Angel star Rod Carew while walking out of Ana-

heim Stadium earlier in the year. Carew greeted Joe before Charboneau had a chance to say a word.

"So you know Rod Carew," Art Charboneau said while smiling at his son. "Now that is something."

One thing Art Charboneau did not find out until much later was that Rod Carew had watched Joe during spring exhibitions and predicted that the Indians outfielder would become the league's top rookie. Carew turned out to be a prophet.

The first rookie award Joe received came two weeks before the end of the season. The Indians were in New York. Joe appeared on the Today Show, where he talked with NBC's Bryant Gumbel. Gumbel told him that he was to be named the network's Rookie of the Year. Interestingly, Joe wore Dan Donnelly's clothes on the show, because he had neglected to pack some of his better outfits for the New York trip.

Cleveland concluded its season with a series at home against the Yankees and then a trip to Baltimore.

That final series against New York was a memorable one. First of all, Joe faced Rich Gossage.

"Gossage is the fastest pitcher I have ever seen," said Joe. "I remember him getting two strikes on me, and then I fouled off a couple of his pitches. Finally, I was called out by the umpire. I turned to him and asked the umpire if the pitch was a strike. He said he thought so. I guess the umpire didn't see the pitch, either."

Charboneau pushed himself extra hard against the Yankees. He wanted to be effective against the elite of the Eastern Division. He also wanted to gain acceptance.

"Earlier in the year, Toronto's John Mayberry used to kid me about the muscles in my arms," said Joe. "He called me Joe Youngblood. He made me feel like a big leaguer by saying things like that. But what really helped me to know that I belonged was my talk with Reggie."

After Joe clouted his mammoth home run in New York, Reggie Jackson approached him during batting practice the next day and asked Joe about the source of his power.

"Where did you get them guns?" Reggie asked Joe. "That home run was not too bad."

While the Yankees were in Cleveland on their last trip, Joe and Reggie met for two hours before a game. The conversation was arranged by Indians Coach Dave Duncan, who is a close friend of Jackson's. Duncan and Reggie were teammates on the Oakland A's.

As the season wound down, Reggie, Duncan, Charboneau and Dan Donnelly sat in the box seats behind the Indians dugout.

"You have to remember one thing," Jackson said to Joe. "You must play for yourself, your manager and your teammates. You can't worry about what the fans say about you. You can be a leader. I think you will be one of the games great players, like Johnny Bench or Pete Rose. You have that kind of ability. In your first year, you have received more acclaim than anyone I can think of. And that includes me. You have the tools to be a superstar, and you can be a big help to the Indians. There is nothing wrong with playing in Cleveland. You can help get them into contention. But there are certain things you have to do."

Then Jackson gave Charboneau these rules to follow:

1. Never accept a drink from a stranger in a bar. They all want to say they were drinking with you, and it will hurt your reputation.

2. Don't throw your helmet and bat where the fans can see them. If you get mad, show your temper privately.

3. Dress nice. Wear a sweater instead of a T-shirt. You are in the limelight, and people are watching how you act. You have to set an example by looking neat.

4. Always run out balls and give 100 percent. Again, remember that people are watching everything you do.

5. Be your own man. Stay clear of parties. You don't have to drink with people or do anything you don't want to.

6. Never rest on your laurels. If you're not hitting or fielding well, come to the park early and work extra on it. You have to strive to get better every day or you won't improve.

7. I make $600,000 a year playing baseball and more than that off the field. Remember, you have to keep your performance up. When you go into a slump, sponsors don't want you to endorse their products. You must play well and hustle, above all else.

"The stuff Reggie said made a lot of sense to me," said Joe. "It was super of him to take the time to talk to me. A lot of players were great to me during the year. Rich Dauer congratulated me at the end of the year for a fine season. Britt Burns and Kirk Gibson were rookies, like me, and they all talked to me a lot and made me feel good. Billy Martin, Rod Carew, Carney Lansford, Doug Corbett, and Rodney Craig are all great guys who spent time with me during the year. I'll never forget that."

Super Joe's final appearance of the season in Cleveland was on October 1st, as the Yankees bombed the Indians, 18–7. Garcia had Joe pinch hit in the bottom of the ninth inning.

"I want you to go up there and bat so these people can give you a standing ovation," said Garcia.

Joe had opened the year by hitting a home run in his second Major-League at bat. Then he went 3-for-3 with a home run in the Tribe's home opener. In that final game with the 19,037 people chanting "Super Joe, Super Joe," Charboneau delivered one more time. On this occasion, it was not a monstrous blast. Rather, it was bloop single to center off former Indians pitcher Gaylord Perry. As Joe limped off the diamond for a pinch runner, he did receive his standing ovation.

Joe finished the year with a .289 batting average along with 23 homers and 87 RBIs. As for the Indians, they ended up in sixth place of the American League East with a 79–81 record.

Afterword

22 ★★★★★★★★

ROOKIE OF THE YEAR

The lights were white, blinding. Joe squinted from the bulbs which never seemed to stop flashing.

This was his day, the day Joe became the American-League Rookie of the Year and the day he made good on a promise to Cindy. His eyes were glazed. He had not slept in two days. But he could not stop smiling.

"Let's face it, winning Rookie of the Year was one of my goals," said Charboneau. "It was five weeks after the season before they announced the rookie award, and I was on pins and needles the last two days. I had been trying to put it out of my mind, but everyone kept asking me about it, and I couldn't help but think about it."

December 2, 1980, was a Tuesday. Joe would learn that he was the league's best first-year player via a late-night telephone call from Jack Lang, the President of the Baseball Writers Association of America.

"That night I couldn't sit still," said Joe. "I was driving Cindy crazy, pacing back and forth. When the call came, I just kept jumping up and down. I was so happy."

Cindy and Joe celebrated by going out to have dinner and champagne. The telephone at their Lakewood condominium rang into the night.

The next morning, an 8 A.M. appearance on a Cleveland radio show was followed by a Stadium press conference. Tribe President Gabe Paul, speaking before a battery of lights, cameras and microphones, said, "I am delighted for Joe. He earned this award. No one handed it to him. There were some people who questioned Joe's fielding as the season progressed, but I want to say that he has worked hard at becoming a Major-League fielder." Joe accepted the honor with an expression of gratitude to his teammates, his coaches and his manager.

Joe had become the third Indian to be so honored. Others were Chris Chambliss in 1971 and Herb Score in 1955. Score, now a Cleveland broadcaster, was present and posed for pictures with Joe. It was noted that Joe was born the year Score won the award.

The suspense surrounding the Baseball Writers Association award had resulted in Joe's being up for the most of two nights. There should have been little tension, however. He was the landslide winner, receiving first place votes on 15 of the 28 ballots, and being chosen second on nine more. Sportswriters who regularly cover Major League baseball voted for the top rookie, ranking their choices in order of preference. Joe received 103 points, compared to 40 for runner-up Dave Stapleton of Boston. Next was Minnesota's Doug Corbett (38 points), Toronto's Damaso Garcia (35), Chicago's Britt Burns (33), Detroit's Ricky Peters (3) and Chicago's Rich Dotson (1). Incredibly, four writers, who must have spent the summer slumped over their typewriters, left Super Joe completely off their ballots.

The Baseball Writers award marked the fifth Rookie of the Year award Super Joe picked off. He had already been honored by the *Sporting News,* Topps, NBC-TV and the Baseball Sportscasters. Joe was at the Indians offices when he learned of the *Sporting News* award. This one is determined by a poll of the players.

The telephone rang in the Tribe's office. The caller wanted to know how to reach Joe Charboneau. The caller was Philadelphia Phillies pitcher Dickie Noles. Noles and Super Joe had played together in Spartanburg during the summer of 1976.

A secretary handed Joe the telephone. "We don't give out the telephone numbers of the players," Joe told Noles.

Noles, unaware of who he was speaking with, became belligerent.

"What do you mean you don't give out numbers?" he repeated. "I'm a ballplayer."

The conversation continued like this for a couple of minutes. Joe finally told Noles who he was speaking to. Noles laughed, then offered his congratulations. "He also told me that he had reminded Dallas Green and other people in the Phillies front office of every home run I hit during the season," said Joe.

The off-season for most professional baseball players is a time of relaxation. For Charboneau, it had become something of a blur. Because he chose to remain in Cleveland for a couple of months following the final pitch of the season, the demands for Joe's time bordered on the incredible.

"I was getting fifteen to twenty calls a day from people asking that he do charity work, alone," said Dan Donnelly. "He couldn't go anywhere in the city without being recognized. In fact, he just may be the most recognizable person in the city of Cleveland."

Super Joe spent countless hours aiding various charities in the area. He was the chairman of the Lung Association. He became involved with Christmas Seals, Spina Bifida and Our Lady of the Wayside. "He just loves kids," said Cindy. "At one time, he said he wanted seven of his own. Then it went up to ten. I'm not too sure about all this. I think someday we might end up adopting some."

It was normal to see Super Joe sitting courtside at a Cleveland Cavaliers basketball game, with a couple of youngsters sitting on his lap. "His patience is unbelievable," said Donnelly. "I've never ever seen him turn anyone away."

Just how much Joe Charboneau meant to many of the youngsters in the Greater-Cleveland area was brought out during the third week of December. A 9-year-old boy was dying of heart disease in a Cleveland hospital. One of his last requests was that he be buried with his autographed picture of Joe Charboneau. He was. "I don't think Joe realized until then just how much influence he has on kids," said Cindy.

The charity work eventually led to Super Joe crossing paths with several of the Cleveland Browns football players. One was tackle Doug Dieken.

On first seeing Dieken, Joe asked Donnelly, "What happened to his face?"

"Shh," Dan said. "That's what happens when you play pro football for ten years."

Dieken, a practical joker of the first degree, made sure he got in his shots at the now-celebrated Indians rookie.

"One minute Doug is cutting you down, and the next minute he's doing something nice. All the times I went to his Monday evening appearances at a Cleveland restaurant, he always made sure to introduce me to the audience," said Joe.

Charboneau wasn't one to back off from a practical joke, either. One night, he and former Browns running back Pat Moriarty were having dinner. The two had become close friends because Donnelly had represented both and they had worked out together. Joe, having eaten dinner, was ready to leave the restaurant. Moriarty wanted to stay. Joe eventually got Pat's attention. He did it by grabbing him by the shoulders and ripping his sport coat in two at the seams.

"Pat couldn't believe it," said Joe. "I got him a new coat, though."

Super Joe's off-season football pals were not limited to the Browns. Donnelly, a longtime friend of Pittsburgh Steelers running back Rocky Bleier, introduced him to Charboneau during the Indians' final series in New York. The two hit it off immediately and Rocky invited the Indians rookie to the Pittsburgh premiere of "Fighting Back," a made-for-television movie based on the book which related the Viet Nam veteran's life, and his courageous return to pro football.

Joe and Dan flew from Cleveland to Pittsburgh on October 23, where they were met by Karen Ahearn, who was Bleier's secretary, and Art Ballant, who became the editor of *Super Joe*. After an enjoyable dinner, they headed to Heinz Hall for the premiere. As the Pittsburgh Pirates of the National League do not play against the American League's Indians, few Pittsburghers would recognize Joe.

There was, however, one person who did walk up to Joe and ask, "Are you Joe Charboneau?"

Super Joe hesitated, then said, "Yes, I am."

The interrogator paused, then came back, "No, you're not, you're just saying that." Sometimes it doesn't matter what you say. You can never win.

A couple of weeks after the premiere of Bleier's movie in Pittsburgh, the Steelers were riding a bus to Cleveland for their annual brawl with the Browns in front of 80,000 Stadium fanatics. Bleier was sitting next to Steelers backup quarterback, Cliff Stoudt. Stoudt, who has known Donnelly for about three years, asked Bleier about him during a casual conversation. Rocky related that Donnelly was doing fine and that he was now representing Indians rookie Joe Charboneau.

Stoudt's eyes got as big as silver dollars. "You're kidding," he said. "Joe Charboneau is my idol. Tell Dan that I would love an autographed baseball, and see if he would have Joe come down to the locker room after the game."

Stoudt, now in his fourth season, made his first start ever in that game against the Browns. Playing for the injured Terry Bradshaw, the former Youngstown State star hit on 18-of-37 passes and totaled 310 yards in a 27-26 loss to the Browns. On this occasion, Art Ballant and Karen Ahearn drove in from Pittsburgh to cheer for the Steelers in enemy territory. They enjoyed watching Joe as he rooted for Rocky and Cliff, even though surrounded by Browns' fans. Joe's popularity was displayed at halftime, as he signed plates, cups and napkins while in line at a concession stand.

Following the game, Joe did visit the Steelers locker room. He was introduced to running back Franco Harris and several other Pittsburgh players by assistant clubhouse man Carl DePhillipo. DePhillipo, nicknamed DiMagg, once chauffeured former Yankee greats Joe DiMaggio and Whitey Ford. Joe left three "Super Joe" T-shirts with Bleier, Harris and Stoudt. The trio have been seen wearing the shirts at Steelers practices.

Harris, the National Football League's third all-time leading runner, behind Jim Brown and O.J. Simpson, also took a liking to Super Joe. The Browns and Steelers met for the second time November 16th in Pittsburgh, and following the game, Franco invited Joe to dinner at his Pittsburgh home. That night, Joe stayed at Stoudt's house. Charboneau later was surprised when Cliff Stoudt attended the luncheon at which the *Cleveland Press* honored him as their Indians Player of the Year.

Super Joe continued to work out daily at St. Edward's High School on Cleveland's west side. He was now bench pressing 330 pounds and running three miles. A series of tests, conducted by Dr. John Bergfeld at the Cleveland Clinic, diagnosed the groin problem as a growth of gristle on the base of his pelvis. Medication was used to dissolve it.

Two days after being named Rookie of the Year by the Baseball Writers Association, Joe was getting ready to work out, when he got a telephone call from Donnelly. Donnelly was at the Indians offices. He had gone there to talk about the possibility of Joe playing winter ball. Tribe General Manager Phil Seghi nearly floored Donnelly when he said, "Why don't we take care of Joe's contract while we're here?" Two hours later, a contract was agreed upon.

Super Joe, who made the minimum of $30,000 in 1980, signed a one-year agreement calling for $90,000. Incentive bonuses could push him to more than $100,000 for the 1981 season.

It had been quite a week for Joe and Cindy Charboneau. First, the Rookie of the Year Award. Then, the contract. "It got to the point where I was on television so much I felt like I was being screened for the movies," said Joe.

There was more. Joe and Cindy had just finalized a deal on a house in Avon Lake, a western suburb of Cleveland. It had four bedrooms, an indoor swimming pool and a nice lot.

"The whole thing has been unbelievable," said Cindy, reflecting on the past year. "Everything just seemed to fall into place." Super Joe Charboneau had indeed come a long way from those nights of boxcar brawling in Santa Clara, California.

Statistics

JOE CHARBONEAU (#34)
Born June 17, 1955
Belvedere, Illinois

Position: Outfielder
Bats: Right
Throws: Right
Height: 6'2"
Weight: 200
Acquired: Traded to Cleveland by Philadelphia Phillies for pitcher Cardell Camper (12/6/78).
Background: Graduated Buchser High School, 1974; played baseball, football and wrestled . . . Attended West Valley Junior College for two years . . . Was team MVP and made All-Northern California team . . . Led Golden Gate Conference in HR . . . Of Canadian-French descent . . . Was drafted No. 2 by the Phillies in the secondary phase of the June 1976 free-agent draft . . . Signed to first contract by Eddie Bockman of the Phillies.
Minor Leagues: Paced '79 AA Chattanooga with a Southern League batting record of .352, the second straight year he set league batting marks (also done at Visalia (.350) in 1978) . . . Was named to S. L. All-Star team . . . Topped Chattanooga with 21 HRs, 78 RBIs and 222 total bases . . . Was second with 24 doubles . . . Named Topps Player of Month for June '79 . . . In addition to hitting .350 in '78, collected five triples, 18 HRs, 34 doubles and 116 RBIs . . . Has fanned just 119 times in 869 at-bats over the past two seasons . . . Has averaged 152.5 hits the last two seasons (a total of 239 games).
Major Leagues: Placed on the Tribe roster 10/18/79.
Personal: Full name Joseph Charboneau . . . Resides in Avon Lake, Ohio . . . Married the former Cindy Engle (1/15/77) . . . Has one child, Tyson, born 9/27/79 . . . Hobbies are camping, fishing, boxing.

209

Playing Record

Year	Club	BA	G	AB	R	H	2B	3B	HR	RBI	BB	SO	SB
1976	Spartanburg	.298	43	121	20	36	3	0	4	18	9	25	1
1977	Peninsula	.172	12	29	4	5	0	0	1	2	4	7	1
1978	Visalia	.350	130	497	119	174	34	5	18	116	76	70	5
1979	Chattanooga	.352	109	372	70	131	24	2	21	78	47	49	6
1980	Cleveland	.289	131	453	76	131	17	2	23	87	49	70	2

Joe Charboneau's Home Runs

No.	Date	Opponent	Pitcher
1	April 11	California	Dave Frost
2	April 19	Toronto	Tom Buskey
3	April 23	Milwaukee	Moose Haas
4	May 9	Seattle	Floyd Bannister
5	May 21	Baltimore	Mike Flanagan
6	May 24	Boston	Jack Billingham
7	May 27	Baltimore	Steve Stone
8	May 28	Baltimore	Jim Palmer
9	June 11	Kansas City	Paul Splittorff
10	June 22	Minnesota	Fernando Arroyo
11	June 28	New York	Tom Underwood
12	July 23	Seattle	Jim Beattie
13	July 23	Seattle	Byron McLaughlin
14	July 25	California	Joje Martinez
15	August 3	Oakland	Matt Keough
16	August 4	Toronto	Paul Mirabella
17	August 16	Milwaukee	Jerry Augustine
18	August 25	Minnesota	Fernando Arroyo
19	August 29	Chicago	Rich Dotson
20	August 30	Chicago	Rich Baumgarten
21	August 31	Chicago	Dewey Robinson
22	September 6	Kansas City	Renie Martin
23	September 26	Baltimore	Mike Flanagan